RETIRE ON RENT

A Proven Systematic Approach to Accumulate Rental Passive Income for Retirement and Financial Freedom

THOMAS TANG

 A catalogue record for this work is available from the National Library of Australia

First published by Ultimate World Publishing 2022
Copyright © 2022 Thomas Tang

ISBN

Paperback: 978-1-922828-65-1
Ebook: 978-1-922828-66-8

Thomas Tang has asserted his rights under the Copyright, Designs and Patents Act 1988 to be identified as the author of this work. The information in this book is based on the author's experiences and opinions. The publisher specifically disclaims responsibility for any adverse consequences which may result from use of the information contained herein. Permission to use information has been sought by the author. Any breaches will be rectified in further editions of the book.

All rights reserved. No part of this publication may be reproduced, stored in or introduced into a retrieval system, or transmitted in any form, or by any means (electronic, mechanical, photocopying, recording or otherwise) without the prior written permission of the author. Any person who does any unauthorised act in relation to this publication may be liable to criminal prosecution and civil claims for damages. Enquiries should be made through the publisher.

Cover design: Ultimate World Publishing
Layout and typesetting: Ultimate World Publishing
Editor: James Salmon

 Ultimate World Publishing
Diamond Creek,
Victoria Australia 3089
www.writeabook.com.au

DEDICATION

For my parents, who, like most Asian parents, worked for their kids more than themselves. They invested most of their time and wealth on their children's education, wanting them to have a better future than themselves. I still remember my mum sitting next to me and encouraging me to study English when I was in year five, even though she did not understand a word. She worked overtime to earn my private tutor fees.

Another big dedication is to two of my uncles, my mum's brothers. They are my role models, true entrepreneurs. They created many successful companies that created thousands of jobs. They are selfless people and made a great contribution to my expensive tuition fees in Australia.

I know they will never ask for me to pay them back, but I will pay back in my own way – to the community and industry and hope everyday Australians can enjoy more financial literacy and ease of retirement.

DISCLAIMER

The information provided in this book is for informational purposes only and should not be construed as financial advice. You should consult with a qualified financial advisor before making any investment decisions.

Donation

10% of the book's revenue will be donated to Rural Education and medical research related charities. This will be publically announced on my website annually.

ACKNOWLEDGEMENT

Thank you to my parents, and uncles, who worked hard to bring the best education opportunities to me and my cousins so that we did not need to suffer the kind of poverty they experienced.

Thank you to my wife, who encouraged and supported me to continue this book while I almost gave up, even during our busiest time after having a first baby girl.

Thank you to my colleagues and friends, who in total ordered 100 copies before I even finished the book. It is a great debt and I need to fulfil the promise. The publication was late, but it eventually arrived as a better version.

I sold 100 copies to my friends before I started my book. This idea was from Natasa Deman, who introduced me to the book writing system as well. I have had 100 'unhappy clients' chasing me for the book for the past five years. Without them teasing me, I wouldn't have been able to finish.

Retire On Rent

I would like to acknowledge my book coach, Melissa Walsh. With her professional weekly coaching and patience in editing, she gave me so much confidence to put my knowledge and experience together in the best possible manner for the readers to digest.

Lastly, to my mentor Lei Feng, who passed so much knowledge in property to me, and opened up so many opportunities for me to create wealth together in the property game.

TESTIMONIALS FOR THOMAS TANG

Many thanks Thomas for your support in navigating property investment and the mortgage market. The guidance Thomas has provided has helped me confidently make investment decisions and I highly recommend this book as a good place to start in developing a property investment plan.

— *Rory McDonald, Coles Executive*

Thomas Tang's book is one of the best I've read on property investment. The author combines a captivating personal story with extensive real estate experience and intimate knowledge of property finance, to produce an entertaining and readable outline of everything people need to know about property investment.

— *Terry Ryder*
Managing Director
Ryder Property Research

'A considered and planned borrowing/lending strategy has been underestimated or ignored by most property investors, however, it is still the No.1 hurdle for property investors to make their next purchase. Most of them only focus on the interest rate of today and lose sight of the bigger picture.

Hence the big banks are always the winners. Only those who are rational and calm enough, can see the true value of a pre-planned and considered loan structure. It is the most critical path for property investors who want to build up their portfolio sensibly, securely and strategically. It is a simple concept, PLAN, including loan options, title ownership, family trust structure, property selection strategies, and so on. The ONLY way is to team up with a panel of selected specialists.

Tom's book has provided a very comprehensive insight and guidance to beginners, a step-by-step guide to achieve financial independence and still sleep at night!'
— *Tim Humphrey is a Veteran in the Mortgage Broking industry with more than 30 years of direct experience from Building Societies to Banking. Being a member of the Australian Armed Forces gave him an understanding of procedures, discipline and planning*

Both Tom and I share the same passion in property game and we both believe in accumulating positive rental income for retirement is an extra layer of safety net. No investment can go without a healthy and sustainable leverage from the banks. His wide strategies have certainly enabled the property investors to overcome many hurdles along the way. A must-read book about lending strategies before your next move in property investment.
— *John Alekoz,*
Builder & Property Developer

Finance and wealth creation is such a complicated and varied topic. There are so many so-called experts clambering for our attention that many simply assign it to the too hard basket.

This book breaks through a great deal of the confusion, bringing a high level of clarity and practicality to the reader, guiding them through the maze of information and helping them to create a clear plan to implement.

Thomas is able to do that by calling on his technical knowledge and real world practical experience, helping people at all levels to achieve financial security and independence.

This book is full of practical tips and tricks and is a must-read for anyone seeking to navigate their way through the finance and wealth creation minefield.

Mark Creedon
Director – Metropole Property Strategists

Tom's passion in the financial matrix is second to none. Sophisticated yet practical knowledge. Value add in building your investment thesis and strategy. Top read of the year!

Annie Mak
Commercial Property Valuer & Uni Teaching Staff

This is a must-read for every serious Australian property investor. Thomas shares his inspiring personal journey and generously shares his framework and blueprint for property investment, most importantly, to the best interests of investors.

You will find the book really speaks to you, because the book helps you navigate through the pitfalls in different stages of the investment lifecycle.

Eric Zhao
Owner of Three Investment Properties & Engineer in Big Five Tech Company

CONTENTS

DEDICATION	III
ACKNOWLEDGEMENT	1
TESTIMONIALS FOR THOMAS TANG	3
PREFACE BY MARK CREEDON	9
CHAPTER ONE: THOMAS – Poverty inspires hard work. "I don't want to be poor again."	13
CHAPTER TWO: THINK AHEAD – How much we need to retire comfortably in Australia	27
CHAPTER THREE: HOW TO SAVE FASTER THAN YOUR BANKS WANT YOU TO KNOW	47
CHAPTER FOUR: THE RISKS OF INVESTING IN PROPERTIES – KNOW THEM BEFORE YOU BUY THEM	71
CHAPTER FIVE: HOLDING COSTS FOR AN INVESTMENT PROPERTY IN AUSTRALIA – SECRETS THE AGENTS WILL NEVER TELL YOU	95

CHAPTER SIX: 18 TACTICS TO PAY OFF YOUR LOAN FASTER – SECRETS THE BANKS WON'T WANT YOU TO KNOW-SHORT TERM — 123

CHAPTER SEVEN: STRATEGIES TO PAY OFF YOUR MORTGAGE FASTER — 157

CHAPTER EIGHT: HOW TO BOOST YOUR BORROWING POWER – ANOTHER SECRET THE BANKS WON'T LET YOU KNOW — 179

CHAPTER NINE: WHAT IS YOUR ENDGAME? — 205

CHAPTER TEN: COMMERCIAL PROPERTY INVESTMENT (DEVELOPMENT OPPORTUNITIES WITH CAPITAL INCOME) IN A NUTSHELL – THE ENDGAME IN PROPERTY INVESTMENT — 241

CHAPTER ELEVEN: CAR LOAN TRAP!! THINK TWICE!! — 263

CHAPTER TWELVE: ESTATE PLANNING WITH PETER LUMB AND STEPH CHAFER — 269

CONCLUSION CHAPTER: FOR A NEW BEGINNING — 285

BONUS CHAPTER: HOW TO GET THE MOST OUT OF YOUR RENTAL PORTFOLIO — 291

ABOUT THE AUTHOR — 301

PREFACE
BY
MARK CREEDON

Property investing, or investing in general, is a mixture of both art and science. On any given Saturday afternoon, around the barbecue with friends and family, you will find investment experts sharing their wisdom.

The problem is that so many of those who are eager to share their wisdom are really little more than theorists. The problem with listening to theorists is that they have no proof. There is nothing to back up their theories and so these are really just opinions – and we all know that saying about everyone having an opinion.

When I was growing up, my parents were hard-working, small business owners who believed that wealth was a bit of a dirty word, and that those providing professional advice on how to grow wealth were in it for the sole purpose of growing their own wealth.

So, as I started my own wealth creation journey, I had to move beyond the limiting beliefs that my parents had instilled in me. Of course, they believed that they were doing the right thing and protecting me and my brothers from unscrupulous spruikers. And by the way, there are plenty of those out there, so there was a good reason my parents wanted to protect us from them.

As I got older I came to realise the difference between theorists and those who actually practice and implement what they preach. As a business coach, I've seen those in business who talk a good game but play a poor one and I've seen those who talk and play a brilliant game.

I think, however, it goes beyond the game you play. The entrepreneurs I have worked with whom I have admired the most have been those who have not displayed a great game but have had at their core a genuine desire to help those around them.

I've watched CEOs commit to building their team, to sharing their wealth and rewarding effort. Where the real difference shines through, though, is in those who go beyond that point and work not just to build the team around them, but to build their entire community.

There is no greater contribution one can make than to seek to lift all those around them, including those who we don't know personally. I've coached CEOs and business owners who have as an integral part of their mission to contribute to their broader community, to help the members in their community to grow and to achieve their hopes and dreams.

Preface

There is almost no greater reward than knowing that you have made a lasting and positive impact on the people around you and that they in turn have been able to share what they learned from you to impact their community.

Of course that is not limited to entrepreneurs. Community leaders, educators, not-for-profit leaders and sometimes even politicians all have the ability to create a very positive impact on the broader community and to use their knowledge and experience to achieve that objective.

It is that very objective that was at the forefront of the reasoning behind Thomas writing this book. Thomas is a successful entrepreneur and property investor, but it wasn't his desire to improve either of those stations in life that prompted the book.

Thomas and I have had many conversations around his genuine interest in helping not just his clients but people in the broader community to achieve their dreams and goals. His interest in providing quality, sustainable finance and investment advice was the catalyst for putting pen to paper in the first place.

So we end up with a book not from a theorist but from someone who has walked that journey and established themselves in both the business and investment worlds.

We have a book that provides honest and open guidelines designed from the very outset to help the reader to improve not just their knowledge but their experience.

Retire On Rent

On that basis, Thomas stands alongside the greatest entrepreneurs and investment advisers I have had the privilege to work with as he brings to fruition his heartfelt desire to help his community and you the reader – to make people more informed and happier, and ultimately improve their lives.

Take this book and learn from it. Apply the principles and guidelines and then do what Thomas has done and share those with your community.

www.retireonrent.au

Free Resources, Tools, Templates and Ongoing Property Market Updates

CHAPTER ONE

THOMAS

"I don't want to be poor again."

To thrive in calamity and perish in soft living; life springs from sorrow and calamity, death comes from ease and pleasure.
— **Confucius.**

Poverty and suffering are some of the best teachers for success. This is something that I know from experience, but neither of them is a destination. There are ways to get out of the cycle, and I will share with you how.

The word 'poverty' touches a nerve in both my mind and my memory. It can mean selling organs, selling kids, low-pay labour, child labour, selling sex for money, motivation to commit crimes. It is happening in almost all developing countries and areas. I have visited many countries and regions. Some were not far from where I have grown up. Some of the above I have witnessed, and hold with lingering fears in my memory.

Let me start by telling you something about my story which will help you along the way. It is something I am very proud of but, more importantly, I understand it is something that everyone can do.

By the time I was 27, I had earnt my first million dollars. This is not including the equity I had used for some properties purchased before. Within three more years in 2021, despite the COVID 19 pandemic, I had built up a property portfolio receiving approximately half a million in passive rental income every year. At the same time, I was able to commit to a lot of public service, volunteer work and pro bono work, and donate money to different charities, mainly related to education and public health research. Despite working very long hours, 80 to 100 on average per week, I still managed to travel internationally twice a year, and be able to contribute to my parents' $100,000 immigration cost. (In Australia, to sponsor your parents from overseas to come to live in Australia with you on a parental sponsor visa, the current cost is approx. $50,000 per person.)

But my life did not begin this way. I was born in a very ordinary family in a small town in China; my family was not so poor and was not so rich. It was average. My father was a police officer, my mum was a pharmacist. However, I had many relatives who were still living in the villages and worked as farmers without any modern machinery support. Buffalo and manual plow on the terrace were all they had. Many farmers in southern China owned only a very small area of terrace. They sold the better parts of rice to the market in the town and kept the lower quality ones for themselves to eat. My mum told me my farmer relatives were poor and did not have enough money to enjoy a modern lifestyle; they were unwilling to spend any money to visit the doctor when they were sick. (It cost them money as China did not have a comprehensive social security system in the 1990s. As of 2010, they now do.) They would work seven days a week to earn the tuition fee for their kids to go to university (university tuition was not free in China).

I only had one Chinese Yuan to spend every day in the '90s as my pocket money (equivalent to AUD 20c), and that was considered a lot among the kids in my town at the time. I could buy a lot of snacks and share them with my mates. My parents used to save up their cash under the bed, and told me again and again that it was for my university tuition fee. Their plan was that I would go to one of the best universities in China, which was Tsinghua or Beijing University, and my life would be successful after that; I could say goodbye to poverty. Chinese parents would blame their embarrassing situation on having never received any tertiary education.

Life is not always as peaceful for everyone. One day an illness visited my family. My father was working too hard and got very sick; it was acute nephritis. It cost all my family's savings, including my university tuition fees, and yet still was not enough. One night, my dad asked me to sit next to his bed. He told me if he left the world, I should look after

Retire On Rent

Mummy like a man. I was seven years old. Unfortunately, at the time we did not have the private insurance system like today. But fortunately, we have close friends and family, and my father's colleagues at the police station. Some people lent the money to us at a very low rate, or no interest. Some just donated whatever they could. My mum took my dad to Shanghai, a more comprehensive hospital that we could not afford without our community's support, to treat my father's illness. Luckily, my father was to fully recover in a year. My mum then became a businesswoman, wanting to earn a lot of money for the family, for my education, and for the family's future, because we did not feel secure enough. In the end, our family encountered bankruptcy almost twice, and went through a long period of depression.

These setbacks during my childhood and puberty actually made me cherish every opportunity and gave me the drive to become financially secure and prepare for the uncertainly in life. It was then that I met a few great mentors in personal growth and business. I learnt to define what is 'enough money' and what is financial sustainability, security, comfort level, and freedom. I also learnt not to be materialistic and to spend humbly (I have never bought a car for more than $20,000 until today).

Luckily for me, due to the tied bonds within the family, two of my uncles who became wealthy sponsored my expensive tuition fees during my study in Australia. The international student fee in Melbourne University was $32,000 on average per student per year between 2011 and 2013. My parents sponsored a small part of my living fees, and then I needed to start working from high school to earn the remaining living fees for myself, including food, tutorial, books and entertainment. Very often I studied for long hours because I didn't want to spend money or go out. I always told myself, as it said in the constitution law in most countries in the world, that once I was over 18, my parents and family would no longer be responsible for my living. I needed to be responsible for myself as an adult.

Many friends asked me why I chose to study in Australia. Why Australia? I guess many Australians could not realise how lucky this land is without visiting many other countries. As I mentioned briefly before, China is overpopulated; people work so hard to fight for limited job opportunities. Even if you work hard, sometimes you are not lucky enough, or you do not have a wealthy family background to support you, and making a living in the modern cities is still very challenging. 'Population pressure', simply put, means that there is not enough air for everybody.

In China, the population is 1.398 billion (2019), while the Australian population is 25.36 million. It is approximately 55 times more.

And yet, Australia has more education resources. Education is actually among the top three 'exports' for the country, number one being mining, number two tourism, and number three education. When Times Higher Education published its annual World University Rankings for 2021, there were six Australian universities ranked within the top 100. The University of Melbourne was the highest-ranked of the Australian contingent at 33 - down from 31 - followed by

Retire On Rent

Australian National University (ANU) and the University of Queensland tied at 54, Monash University at 57, the University of Sydney at 58 and the University of New South Wales (UNSW) at 70.

China, with 55 times more people, has only six universities within Times Higher Education Ranking Top 100, those being Tsinghua University (20), Peking University (23), Fudan University (70), University of Science and Technology of China (87), Zhejiang University (94) and Shanghai Jiao Tong University (100). It's not that the people are not smart enough - in fact, they are all very smart. The ranking was not measured by students' or teachers' IQ, but rather by research contribution. Basically, it takes into account the history of the university, and human resources. Simply put, because of the significantly higher population in China, it did not matter how hard I worked, there was very little chance for me to get into Tsinghua University (20) or even Fudan University (70), yet I managed to get into the University of Melbourne (31). And for a lot of my childhood friends in China who did not get into the universities in China, and who didn't have the advantage of a rich family background, they ended up as low-pay labour.

It feels like yesterday that they were seated next to me. Some of them were smarter than me, and some worked harder than me.

The journey to Australia was not easy. The Immigration Department delayed my student visa application for a year since I was born in Fujian Province in China, a region famous for smuggling people who came from very poor and small villages. I really understand those people, feel sympathy for some, even admire them. They would risk their lives for prosperity for their family because poverty is almost a death sentence for a lot of them.

Something that is worthwhile mentioning is that the word 'Casino' came from the dialogue from Fujian's capital city, Fuzhou. It means 'Let the game (gambling) begin'. What an adventurous spirit. In fact, the poorer the people are, the higher their risk tolerance, because they have nothing to lose at the beginning.

Back to my first day in Melbourne, and everything was fresh. People looked the same to me as well, just as they say all Asians look the same. The Aussie accent was so strange to me, as only American and British accents were taught in China. I loved the fresh air and blue sky here. The birds were not afraid of me, and would get close to me to ask for food, perhaps. If these birds were in China, they could be the food in the night market very soon.

My parents gave me AUD $20,000 cash; they were so worried about sending their only son too far away, without any relatives there, and they could not help me with anything. $20,000 Australian dollars was equivalent to my dad's salary for three years. And I lost it. From the house I first stayed at in Melbourne, on the way to the bank to open my first bank account, I lost the money my parents had given me. When I sat down in front of the banker, I took out my passport, and opened the account. And then she asked me, 'How much would you like to put in today, Sir?' I searched my pack and pockets, inside and out. My mind went blank - I had just lost three years of my father's salary.

I felt like a piece of my heart was missing. I could not sleep for days. I did not tell my parents, because I knew they would feel more heartbroken than me. They had hardly spent any money themselves to save this up for me. I decided to look for work even though at the time I could not speak fluent English. I knocked on many doors, got rejected, and finally found a job at a Chinese restaurant in Mitcham called Yummy King, working as a kitchen hand. I started on a low hourly rate because I was so new, with no working experience and could not speak English very well at that time. But the boss, chief and staff were so patient and nice to me. They prepared quick and delicious dinners for the staff before the restaurant opened at night, and very often the chef spoiled me with a lunch box for my school next day. It was so comforting to be loved by someone outside your country town. The chef was a Vietnam-born Chinese refugee. His grandfather was a war refugee from China to Vietnam after WWII. And they were not welcome during the Cold War, so he and his family became refugees again and came to Australia.

To save money, I bought a secondhand bike to ride to school from home to save the expensive cost of taking the bus. I guess it was a good thing, 20 minutes to school and 20 minutes back, free exercise. I bought a shaver from the $2 shop, and never visited a barber (until today). I bought the 'expire soon' food from the supermarket, and at one point, I could almost tell the 10c difference for an item between Coles and Woolworths. Since my student visa limited me to only

Thomas

20 hours PAYG salary work per week, I started selling items on eBay as a self-employed person as well. The hours were not restricted being self-employed.

I realised that if I spoke better English, my hourly rate as a casual employee at work would increase in the market, so I worked damn hard to learn English. I read the newspaper out loud at home and attempted to memorise more than 100 words every day, but only ten of them remained in my mind the next day. Still, it worked time after time. I watched the American series 'Friends' alone, and for every sentence they said, I pressed the 'pause' button and repeated after their lines. For the lines I liked from the movies, I wrote them down to memorise. I almost memorised the film 'The Shawshank Redemption' once. I learnt to sing many English songs to improve my pronunciation. I hated the subject English when I was in China because I thought I would never need to use it in China anyway. But there was no choice in Australia, every subject was based on English (except the subject Chinese as First Language). The hard work paid off - in Year 12, not only did I get into the school debating team as an international student from a non-English speaking country, but I also represented the school in the Victoria High School Debating Competition and won the Excellent Debater Award.

I worked so hard because I knew the tuition fee was expensive for international students. I did not want to become a burden to my parents and uncle. So, I did the work I could, such as tutoring, pizza delivery, librarian, eBay sales, door knocking sales, translator - I did them all. I took summer and winter school during my university time as well, while many others were enjoying a long holiday overseas with their parents' money (nothing wrong with that, I was not jealous). I almost managed to finish my three-year degree in two years; for the sake of my 'three years university visa term,' I had to put on two elective and easy-going subjects in my final year of uni. But that left a lot of time for me to do more business and internships to prepare for 'real life' after uni.

I did not even turn up to my graduation - for me, it was a total waste of time and money, and unnecessary to pay for all the photos and graduate dress, and listen to someone's speech when I could watch better ones on YouTube. Holding a big graduation certificate is no different from holding a big invoice that is not tax deductible. I simply wanted to leave uni ASAP to get a full-time job and earn a living, earn money to be able to afford my parents' immigration to Australia.

Then one day, I got an internship from the Bank of Melbourne, and realised my passion for the banking service. I went from an intern to a teller, to a personal banker, to a lending officer, and ultimately went on to become a national award-winning mortgage broker business owner. I could now afford to pay my parents $20,000 Australian dollars a year daily living fee while they may not be able to work. I married, bought my dream home, volunteered, and donated, and shared strategies with people who want to take control of their personal finance. I was finally living the dream.

I coached more than 30 brokers to be successful and independent. I have also helped thousands of Australian families to move into their dream homes.

Thomas

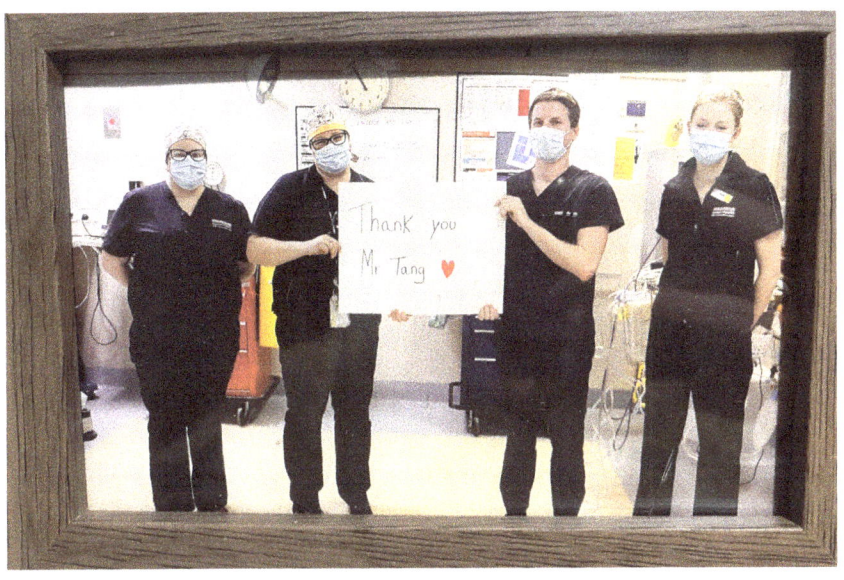

Donation to a few hospitals during COV-19, a thank you photo from Eastern Health

A dream home me and my wife purchased in Victoria with a large vegie garden for healthy living.

Retire On Rent

I am lucky because I have found my passion. There is a proverb in old French, 'How to be rich? Do what you like, and the money will come.'

My passion is to help more people to get out of financial anxiety like my family suffered before and start to enjoy their lives with true financial security, or even freedom. I work long hours, but I never feel like I am working. With this experience and passion, the industry can be changed together, and we can finally see a world without poverty.

Come with me on the journey to a better life as I share with you my strategies, property investment insights and industry secrets. I believe that real wealth can be shared - not just the few dollars I have in my pocket. As Warren Buffet believes, 'The real wealth cannot be stolen away, such as your happiness, memories with family and knowledge'.

Thomas

QUESTIONNAIRE

1. Have you ever struggled financially?

_____

_____

_____

2. How did you get to that place?

_____

_____

_____

3. Do you often have nightmares about fears of poverty, and uncertainty? If so, describe that fear and dream context.

_____

_____

_____

4. If you were to win a $10,000,000 lottery, how would you like to spend the money?

_____

_____

_____

_____

5. What makes you happy in life? For those related to materialism, there is nothing wrong with that. Write them down and see how much it will cost you. It might be a holiday to Rome, going on safari in Africa, buying a dream car, a dream house, going back to uni to study again, buying your parents their dreams, etc. (Things with a price tag in life are easy goals. Those without the price tags are the hard ones. So, let's start with the easy goals first.)

_____

_____

_____

_____

CHAPTER TWO

THINK AHEAD

How much we need to retire comfortably in Australia.

The world heads into a crisis every seven to ten years. It could be a financial crisis, it could be COVID-19. That's why it's so important to never rely on the pension fund or government for retirement, and I have discovered a way to do exactly that. Don't plan your retirement from your 40s, like most people do. We should plan your retirement from 18, or 21. As early as possible. And it is never too late.

<u>To begin, let's answer the question: what is the meaning and definition of wealth?</u>

There are many definitions of wealth, and every individual will think it is a different thing. For the purpose of thinking ahead, let's first work backwards and ask the question; what is enough to look after our own retirement?

Retire On Rent

When I was working as a teller in the bank, there were two kinds of retirees; one came in and took out their pension for daily necessary spends, with a worried look on their face. The other one came in happily, smiling and calm, and took out the rental income without debt to buy coffee and yum cha for themselves, and gifts for the grandchildren.

When thinking about your future and the kind of "wealth" you would like to have, ask yourself this question: do you want to rely on a payment from Centrelink for your financial survival, or would you like to have some money put aside by thinking ahead?

Centrelink is important and an essential part of our social welfare. It prevents people from dying in poverty, suffering depression from poverty, reduces rates of crime and domestic violence, provides humanity support - all the good things.

However, it only provides the minimum and often leaves people living with scarcity, unable to do the things they would like to. At worst, it does not give enough to pay the bills. This is because these people have not thought ahead and saved for their own future.

Surviving is not enough. Life is beautiful, and Australia provides us a fair chance to get wealthy and enjoy life fully. If we always settle for 'just enough' in our bank account, without emergency funds and personal investment in assets, we will soon be poor again when a crisis visits, whether it is COV-19, COV-29, or COV-39. We could encounter any misfortune, such as a car accident, company closure, or redundancy. You may find one of your family friends, or relatives coming to you at a low point of their lives and needing your financial support, or needing you to give up your current job and income to sacrifice some time to accompany them, for example, to be a family carer for your elderly parents.

There are many things in life that we can enjoy nowadays, and many of them come with a price. I am not talking about materialistic items, such as expensive watches or cars, although there is nothing wrong with that if you can easily afford them. What I am talking about is time to spend with your family and time to explore the world. Free time is one of the benefits of wealth, and wealth comes from thinking ahead. Imagine having free time to do a lot of exercise, having free time not to work for a couple of months and accompany your wife on a honeymoon in Europe or China. Having free time to care for your unwell family member because you don't need to work for a year. Imagine travelling the world with that year off just because you can.

All of these things are possible if you think ahead. You just need to start your investment journey as soon as possible, let it build, and reap the benefits.

The Association of Superannuation Funds of Australia's (ASFA) estimate of how much money you'll need in retirement, depending on your lifestyle.

ASFA Retirement Standard	Annual living costs	Weekly living costs
Couple – modest	$40,829	$782
Couple – comfortable	$62,828	$1,203
Single – modest	$28,254	$541
Single – comfortable	$44,412	$850

Source: ASFA Retirement Standard, March quarter 2021

In the years of looking after clients' personal finances and families' wealth, I have concluded that there are three categories of wealth:

1) Health status: physical, mental, and spiritual health. Show appreciation, seek self-improvement, do not blame society or say that life is not always fair. We also don't want to be the one who works so hard to earn a lot of money, that in the end they have no life to spend it on. We don't want to spend all our earnings on hospital bills because we haven't looked after our health. Rich people invest their time and money in maintaining a good health status in order to cope with long hours of work and the challenges that may come along.

2) Meaningful relationships with people around you: you do not want to be rich and have no friends, right? Isolation and loneliness also cause problems for our mental health. This can also include social status. Some people obtain a sense of achievement from being respected and being appreciated, which may include meaningful relationships such as with our parents, children, colleagues, friends, and clients.

3) Financial status: of course, this is not all this book is about. Property investment is only one of the traditional segments under personal finance and investment options, out of many. Money is not the only way to obtain happiness but having a sense of 'enough' will provide the basic needs for security. We will have

enough money to exchange for sufficient food, shelter, a warm room, warm food during the winter, and warm hugs from your loved ones. Material needs are there to enhance our sense of security as well. Money does not buy you happiness, but it is the foundation of many other meaningful experiences in our lives. Furthermore, I would like to appeal to the industry and society, a new definition about financial wellbeing. It is based on how much money you have, how well you can save and manage your money, and financial literacy and attitude towards money. So rather than how rich is a country, we need to measure how financially happy is a country.

Now let's take a look at the three levels of 'rich'. Which category would you like to aim for?

- Level one: financially secure (or financial independence). One does not need to take any low-income support payment from Centrelink. He or she can work independently to earn a basic living for themselves, such as paying for food, housing (mortgage or renting), amenities, and limited entertainment expenses. This category can afford domestic travel, but perhaps does not have air conditioning in the summer or heating during winter. There are no extra savings.

- Level two: financial comfort. One has some extra savings after the basic living expenses. Can afford international travel, and to buy generous gifts for family and friends. This category is able to make contributions of monetary donations and has spare time to do regular volunteer work without worrying about his or her finances. This category can afford some luxury items, such as a car worth more than $150,000, international travel, modern and smart home system, private health insurance cover, children's private school fees, etc.

- Level three: financial freedom. One can live comfortably without working actively at work or from his or her business. My hope is this book can help you to get there faster and safer.

Let me say this: money will not make you a better or worse person. It just enlarges one's character.

If someone can show you how to get rich easily, why choose to remain comfortable only? As I explained before, being rich and wealthy means you have more than enough for both the unknown crisis ahead, and for enjoying life to the fullest potential. Furthermore, you can leave a legacy to the next generations (although they probably can earn more than you).

And I really want to remind you about the power of inflation. I know it is not something we think about very often, but it does have an effect on our quality of life. Inflation will soon push your comfortable level down to the base line and force you into survival mode again. If you spend some time to look up the key word 'inflation' in Google, YouTube, Tik Tok, Twitter, you will find many scary facts. You see, inflation is a thing that is out of our control. How it works is the government prints money as fast as possible to compensate for the problems they have created, such as starting a war with no economic benefits, or giving out too much Centrelink money to win the votes. However, this is money the government simply cannot afford without raising the government debt. Without too much economic theory explanation and argument, the result is that our purchasing power is not catching up with the house prices, or the cost of goods and services.

Think of it this way: if our salary only increases 3%-5% but inflation increases by 11% for example, our quality of living decreases significantly. The images below are a good illustration of inflation.

The first image (pg 35) indicates the price increases for many essential products, such as the price of bacon, which increased by 11% on average from July 2020 to July 2021. The price of beef increased by 8%. Lettuce increased by 5%. Fish increased by 7%. Milk increased by 8%. All these are essential food costs. On average, let's say food price increases by 8% each year.

There are also some other costs, such as airfares, hotel, petrol, which may all fluctuate significantly due to COV-19.

Let us assume in 30 years' time, that if your salary is $100,000 today, and increases by 5% on average per year, then compounding the increase rate, your salary will be estimated around $432,194.24 per year before tax.

Retire On Rent

Assuming your living expense is $20,000 per year for you as a single man or woman, if it increases by 8% per year compounding the increase rate, your living expense will become $201,253.14 in 30 years' time. It is almost half of your income before tax.

If we assume the tax rate remains unchanged, your income after tax will be $246,882.67. Minus your basic living expenses, this will equal around $45,000. Maybe $45,000 cannot buy much in 30 years' time.

How scary is it to think about this? With just 3% difference in inflation, we can lose significant purchasing power in 30 years' time. This is the power of compounding, and the power of time.

Check out the following images…..

Think Ahead

INFLATION FROM JULY 2020 TO JULY 2021

BACON	↑ 11%
BEEF	↑ 8%
LETTUCE	↑ 5%
FISH	↑ 7%
MILK	↑ 8%
AIRFARE	↑ 19%
GASOLINE	↑ 42%
DRESSES	↑ 19%
HOTELS	↑ 24%
USED CARS	↑ 42%

A snapshot of summaries for the CPI increased from different websites. There is an idiom in Chinese called 'Yi-Shi-Zhu-Xing' which summaries the four main categories of basic necessities of spending. 'Yi' means clothing, 'Shi' means food, 'Zhu' means shelter (housing), 'Xing' means traveling.

Retire On Rent

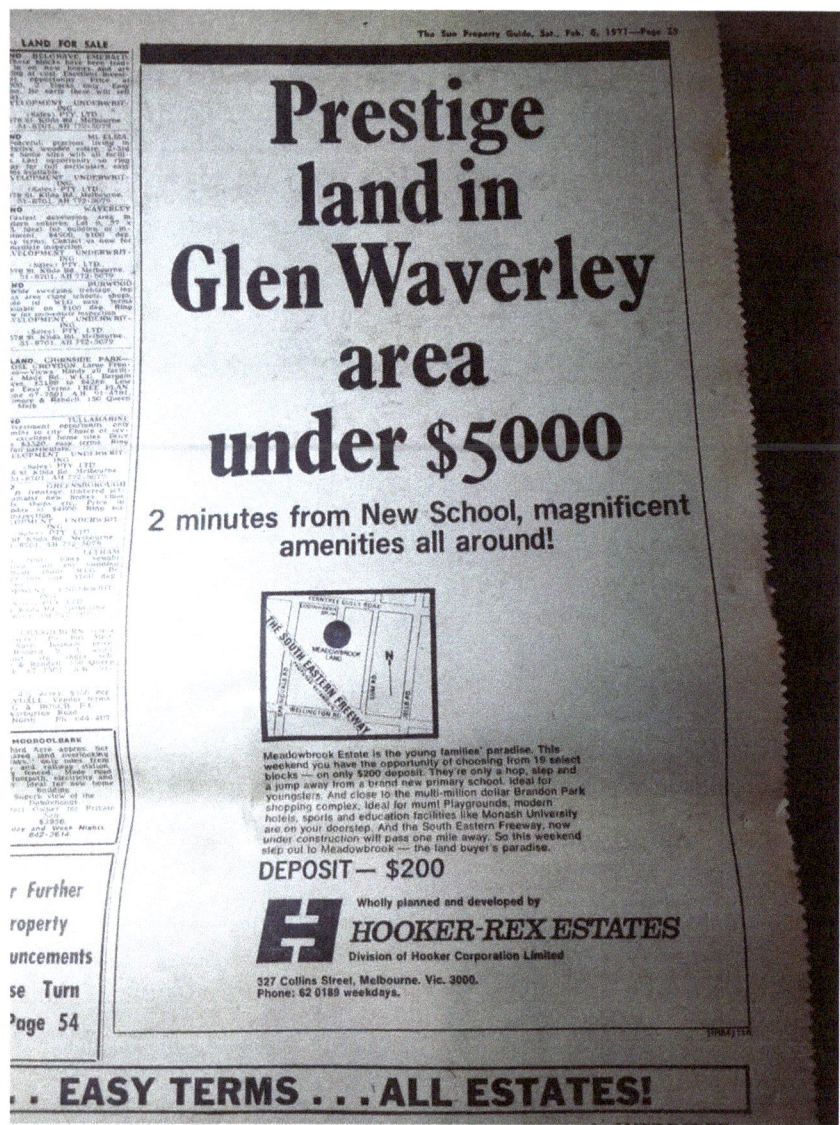

The salary could have been very different before, but please remember, one of the reasons is the governments have never stopped printing money - it does not matter if they were doing it slowly or fast. Investment sometimes is a MUST, not a choice. Otherwise, you will be losing the money you earn and may not be able to keep your wealth.

Think Ahead

On the other hand, let's look at the newspaper in 1971, specifically an advertisement to sell land. Today when I am writing this chapter, we are in 2021, it is 50 years later. The median price is around $1.5 million today. Compare with the vacant land worth $5,000 40 years ago, it's multiplied 300 times!!! Isn't property investment something safe and profitable? People just lose patience with property investment and are more interested in get rich quick schemes.

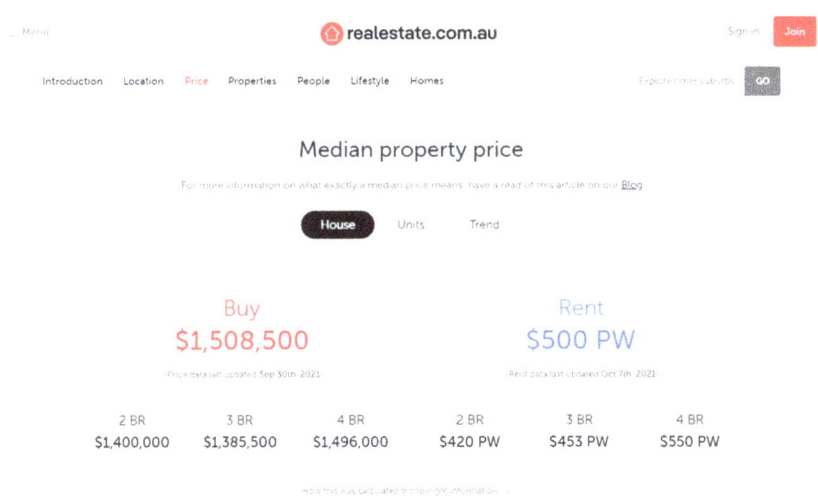

The fact is we cannot prevent the banks from printing money, and the inflation rate is beyond our control. The governments and big corporations are only designing the lifestyle to allow us to be comfortable today. But what is comfortable today, may be very unaffordable after decades.

That's why I would like to encourage you to all think ahead as early as possible. Put some money aside and keep investing in something safe that carries long-term, sustainable growth. Let's imagine beyond being financially secure and financially comfortable - let's aim for financial freedom. And it is absolutely possible. We have often overestimated what we can achieve in a short period of time but underestimated what we can accomplish over a longer-term period.

In this book, I would like to share with you as much of my knowledge of property investment principles and strategies as possible. My team's mission is to build the property investment community and provide ongoing support with the lowest cost possible to all who want it so badly and can commit their own long-term goals.

WHAT ARE THE FACTORS THAT DECIDE IF YOU WANT TO BE COMFORTABLE OR RICH ETC?

Being comfortable is a dangerous status. You may have heard of the 'Boiling Frog' effect. It is a fable describing a frog being slowly boiled alive. The premise is that if a frog is put suddenly into boiling water, it will jump out, but if the frog is put tepid water which is then brought to a boil slowly, it will not perceive the danger and will be cooked to death.

Maybe it is a lucky thing to have once suffered during my childhood. My parents were too comfortable with their position at the time, and it wasn't until a few challenges visited our family that we learnt how easy it was to lose almost everything we had.

Think Ahead

WHAT ARE THE DIFFERENT WAYS TO AIM TO BE COMFORTABLE OR RICH?

We all need to think ahead to our retirement from the age of 18, or as early as possible. The average life expectancy in Australia is around 82.90 as of 2019. If we retire at around 60 years old, we have 22.90 years remaining, and is our saving really enough for us to live without consistent income? If we just rely our retirement expenses on the cash savings in the bank account we withdraw from our superannuation, the savings rate in the bank account is always lower than the inflation growth.

Speaking of superannuation, some people believe super was not designed for retirement. They believe it was designed to reduce economic growth and limit wage increases, and that is what it does. In fact, I personally do not believe the big superannuation funds have the best interest of my retirement at heart. The fees and charges are high - it costs a lot of money to hire a nice office for them to work there with high wages.

Of course, there are many ethical superannuation companies out there, but my point is, we should take control of our own retirement planning, and not let the superannuation and quickly-running-out government pension to be fully responsible for our own precious retirement.

The best investment most people make in Australia is their principal place of living. By holding it for decades, the price multiplies, and they pay off their mortgage through their hard-earned dollars. Time and inflation ensures the value of their home multiples, and the ATO and SRO (State Revenue Office) charge no capital gains tax when they are selling their home. For example, you purchased a house at Glen Waverley in Victoria in 1971 for $10,000, and 40 years later when you retire, you sold it for $1.5 million. If there is no mortgage already, you are earning $1.49 million net profit with $0 tax!!!!

Of course, I am also assuming you skip the almost 50% divorce rate in Australia.

But guess what is stopping most young people from getting into their first home? It is the savings. People buying their first home on average in Australia are aged between 33 and 36, from different studies. It means that when people graduate from uni or TAFE study at the age of 21, it takes people more than ten years to save up! Who should we blame? Afterpay? The buy now, pay later concept? The easy to approve, hard to pay off high interest rate at 24% for personal loans and credit cards? The advertisements promoting materialism?

Here are some fun facts and infographic done by the property agent company Ray White, with data collected by CoreLogic.

Think Ahead

Home ownership is an aspiration held by many in Australia, as it provides security and long-term financial benefits. In fact, the Australian Bureau of Statistics (ABS) found that our nation has one of the highest levels of home ownership in the world, staying at around 70 per cent the last 40 years.

Retire On Rent

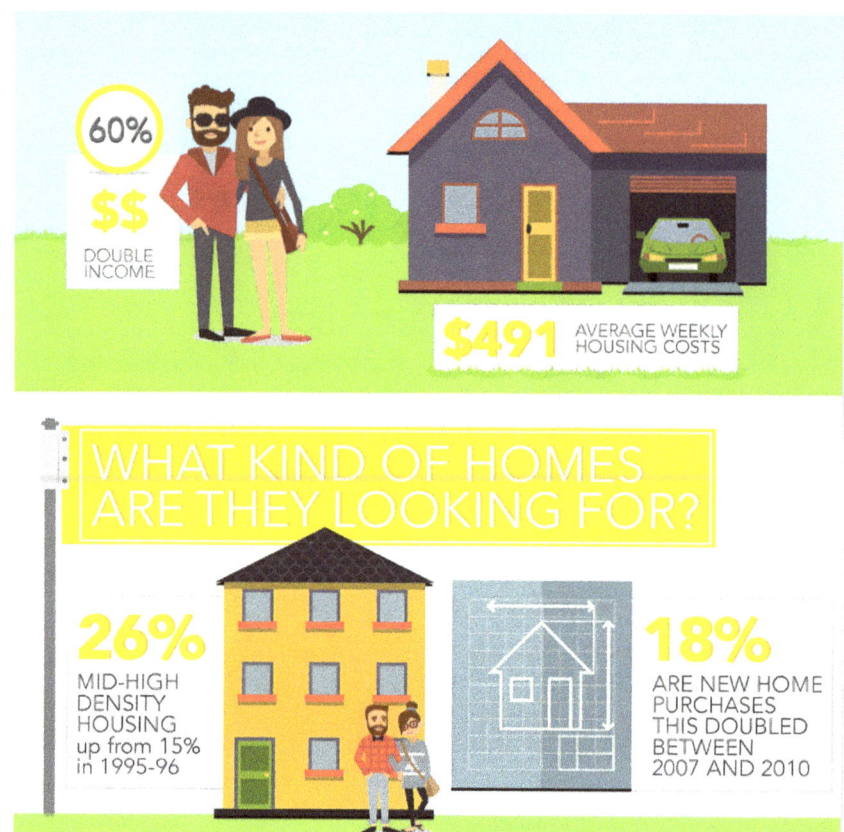

From: https://raywhiteruraltweedvalley.com.au/news/infographic-first-home-buyers

https://www.realestate.com.au/news/average-age-of-aussie-first-home-buyers-closer-to-40-than-20-research-reveals/

And guys, please do not dream of getting the pension from the government. It is like a social security safety net, but not for a comfortable retirement lifestyle. A lot of people take the pension and fly to Thailand or Bali for cheaper living costs (this is not a retirement tip).

Think Ahead

And if you like children, and grandchildren, make sure you die as a rich grandfather or grandmother. I enjoy imagining the moment when my kids and grandkids are seated around my sick bed in the best aged care facility in Australia, or in a private hospital, or maybe my own bedroom at home, listening to me and my lawyer announce my Estate of Will, and one of the conditions is that……. I am only joking. I am sure we would prefer to be remembered as a great person rather than for our money. But leaving some extra savings to support the kids' home deposit to get into the property market earlier will be a nice thing to do.

Occasionally, let the family dinner be a 'Money Talk' Session, and talk about money. It is not a shameful topic, but it is a shame to not talk about it. Teaching your kids about how to plan ahead, think ahead, walk the talk, self-discipline, and wealth mindset is a good thing. Talk about the tax rate, banks' products, insurance, news about the economy, books about personal finance, and ask them what they think - what would they do with their money.

EXERCISE

Walk through a cemetery and look at the headstones there. Think about your future and the unavoidable reality that life is short. Think of the life you would like to lead and what you want to leave to future generations.

"LIFE IS SHORT, HAVE YOU PLANNED OUT FOR YOUR LIFE? HAVE YOU FULLFILLED IT? FOR FURTHER GENERATIONS?"

QUESTIONNAIRE

1. How did you feel after visiting the cemetery?

   _____

   _____

2. Did it scare you or inspire you to think ahead, or both?

   _____

   _____

Think Ahead

3. Did it make you think about what legacy you would like to leave your family?

_____

_____

4. Did it make you think about the type of life you would like to lead?

_____

_____

_____

5. What areas of your life do you think ahead in? Is it health, wealth, relationships etc?

_____

_____

_____

6. Did you come from a family that thought ahead? Did you see your parents planning for their retirement?

_____

_____

_____

_____

7. At what age did you start thinking about the future and what you wanted for your retirement? Is this the first time you have thought about it?

_____

_____

_____

_____

CHAPTER THREE

HOW TO SAVE FASTER THAN YOUR BANKS WANT YOU TO KNOW

How to save up fast for your deposit

How to refinance & cash out for your next investment property

The number one mistake most parents make when it comes to financial literacy for their kids is advising them to put the money in their savings accounts — FOREVER. In the world of debt, and with money printing faster than ever, this is an old concept that is making most people financially disadvantaged. In my older generations, I have seen people use cash to buy properties, never use loans and put all their cash in the bank account for 50 years. Even my grandparents did that too, putting cash under their bed. This breaks my heart because while their money is sitting there idly, inflation is causing their costs to constantly rise.

The fact is, 'Savers are losers'. Sounds harsh I know, but let me explain:

We must beat the CPI and inflation rate. When we have cash in our hands, since the banks are printing new money out of our control, it is disadvantageous to most of our lives. In a nutshell, the longer you hold the cash in hand, the more value and purchasing power it will lose. Imagine you spent 40 hours a week to earn $1,000, and you put that $1,000 in your bank savings account for two years. If it loses its value by 5% per year due to inflation, and 10% over two years, that means its purchase power will be less than $900. At the end of the day, this means your time is stolen. 10% of that 40-hour work week is four hours that you can never take back. Four hours per week means 108 hours per year. 24 hours per day, and 4.5 days you lost. Most people do not even use four hours per week to study about financial literacy.

Isn't that scary to think about? A lot of my friends who work in the investment bank sector believe that the real CPI will never be published and captured - it is much higher than the facts. Just simply looking around, you can see the CPI on Australian government website (ABS) is 1.3% this quarter (on 1st of March 2022), but the growth of house prices in most capital cities is above 7% per year. The car price increased by close to 30%, and people buying groceries for the family almost doubled their costs in the past two years of inflation. I may need to increase the price of my book.

How To Save Faster Than Your Banks Want You To Know

Inflation, the history of printing money, and how the bank system is set up are complex topics. I want to recommend to you the book 'The Currency Wars' by Song, if you are interested in learning more about them.

According to the book, Western countries in general, and the United States in particular, are controlled by a clique of international bankers, who use currency manipulation (hence the title) to gain wealth by first loaning money in USD to developing nations and then shorting those countries' currency. You can read more about it here: https://en.wikipedia.org/wiki/Currency_Wars

We must learn to invest and use the loan as leverage from a young age. What is the better alternative? I want to emphasise that this is not financial advice. This is my personal experience that may not be suitable to everyone.

So what are the better saving alternatives?

1. Other banks' saving accounts: Do your research and compare. There are many new banks today, or banks that need savings clients more desperately. Today, in March of 2022, most people's savings accounts have less than 0.5% return. Traditionally, banks will give a low saving rate to existing customers and give the new clients higher saving rate for usually a three-month period. Usually, the bank will have a type of savings account that will give you a first three-month honeymoon period for a 1% extra higher rate. I have seen clients move banks every three months to roll over their lump sum savings.

Be careful with some of the terms and conditions though. For example, with some accounts, if you withdraw the money within the same month, you lose the bonus interest rate. Do online transfers to avoid fees and choose the banks that charge no fees or lower fees.

Most of your bankers will only tell you their promotions. You need a subject matter expert to provide advice, or you need to read the fine print thoroughly.

There are many small new banks now, such as ING, which is ATM-free for all of Australia, $0 fee, and generally higher savings rate than major banks. Other new competitors include 86400, the first Australian smart bank and a full digital bank with an app that can also analyse your spendings and saving patterns. Up Bank, U Bank, VOLT, Macquarie, etc. are other examples.

2. Term deposit: Even though it is a low savings rate nowadays, this is still a good option for those who want to practise their discipline around not touching money and controlling overspending. However, the fixed rate is not as attractive as it was in previous years.

3. Now, let's get offensive to the banks. Index funds, ETFs, or management funds. These are not savings accounts; they are investment options. There is always risk associated with investment. But the key is to understand them and understand your own risk tolerance. By choosing a reputable brand with good reviews and long history, you are mitigating the risks.

Definition of Index Fund: An index fund is a mutual fund or exchange-traded fund designed to follow certain pre-set rules (such as low turnover, low trading, low risk exposure), so that the fund can track a specified basket of underlying securities as investments.

Basically, this is where you put the money for someone to manage on your behalf; he or she will choose different stocks on ASX 200 or bonds to mix it up as a portfolio. The fund manager is an expert and does this daily. For me, this is a better option, rather than picking the stock individually, when I don't know what the best time is to buy and sell. My time is worth a lot more doing my own job.

Definition of ETFs (Exchange-traded Fund): An exchange-traded fund is a type of investment fund and exchange-traded product, i.e. they are traded on the stock exchange. They have a lot in common with index funds, but are more specific and more flexible. With the index fund you are investing in the whole market (i.e., ASX200), while with ETFs you are buying a specific segment of the market.

There are different types of ETFs. Sometimes people prefer to invest in ETFs because they long that industry. (Long: you believe it will grow in the long-term. Short: you believe it will fall in the long-term.)

Different Types of Exchange-Traded Funds

Bond ETFs invest in a basket of bonds, such as municipal, state, federal, and corporate bonds

Industry ETFs track industry sectors, such as technology, pharmaceuticals, or energy

Commodity ETFs invests in physical commodities, such as oil, agricultural goods, or natural resources

Currency ETFs invests in global currencies, such as the U.S. dollar, Euro, or Japanese Yen

Inverse ETFs use a variety of derivatives to make a profit from a decline in the value of a stock by shorting them

(source: Mint Intuit)

I will use Vanguard as an example, one of the most popular funds for index, ETFs, and management fund. Note that I do not get any commission from this example.

How To Save Faster Than Your Banks Want You To Know

Average annual total returns as at 31 Jan 2022

+ Add to compare		Type	Fees p.a.	1 year	3 years p.a.	5 years p.a.	10 years p.a.	66 products available
⊕ Compare	Vanguard Conservative Index Fund VAN0108AU	Managed fund	0.29%	+2.43%	+5.60%	+5.20%	+6.01%	>
⊕ Compare	Vanguard Diversified Conservative Index ETF ASX: VDCO	ETF	0.27%	+2.44%	+5.62%	—	—	>
⊕ Compare	Vanguard Balanced Index Fund VAN0109AU	Managed fund	0.29%	+5.35%	+8.01%	+7.60%	+8.08%	>
⊕ Compare	Vanguard Diversified Balanced Index ETF ASX: VDBA	ETF	0.27%	+5.37%	+8.03%	—	—	>
⊕ Compare	Vanguard Growth Index Fund VAN0110AU	Managed fund	0.29%	+9.90%	+10.28%	+8.84%	+9.54%	>
⊕ Compare	Vanguard Diversified High Growth Index ETF ASX: VDHG	ETF	0.27%	+14.03%	+12.66%	—	—	>
⊕ Compare	Vanguard Active Emerging Market Equity Fund VAN0221AU	Managed fund	1.045%*	+0.88%	—	—	—	>
⊕ Compare	Vanguard Active Global Credit Bond Fund VAN3932AU	Managed fund	0.40%	-2.38%	—	—	—	>
⊕ Compare	Vanguard Active Global Growth Fund VAN0722AU	Managed fund	0.6825%*	+4.10%	—	—	—	>
⊕ Compare	Vanguard Australian Corporate Fixed Interest Index ETF ASX: VACF	ETF	0.20%	-2.54%	+2.78%	+3.38%	—	>

	Fund	Type	Fee	1yr	3yr	5yr	10yr	
Compare	Vanguard Australian Corporate Fixed Interest Index Fund VAN0065AU	Managed fund	0.24%	−2.87%	+2.75%	+3.35%	−	>
Compare	Vanguard Australian Fixed Interest Index ETF ASX: VAF	ETF	0.15%	−3.65%	+2.11%	+2.84%	−	>
Compare	Vanguard Australian Fixed Interest Index Fund VAN0001AU	Managed fund	0.19%	−3.69%	+2.07%	+2.81%	+3.82%	>
Compare	Vanguard Australian Government Bond Index ETF ASX: VGB	ETF	0.20%	−3.89%	+2.11%	+2.85%	−	>
Compare	Vanguard Australian Government Bond Index Fund VAN0025AU	Managed fund	0.24%	−3.93%	+2.06%	+2.76%	+3.69%	>
Compare	Vanguard Australian Inflation-Linked Bond Index Fund VAN0064AU	Managed fund	0.29%	+1.41%	+4.67%	+4.23%	−	>
Compare	Vanguard Australian Property Securities Index ETF ASX: VAP	ETF	0.23%	+19.63%	+7.48%	+8.70%	+12.27%	>
Compare	Vanguard Australian Property Securities Index Fund VAN0004AU	Managed fund	0.23%	+19.68%	+7.49%	+8.70%	+12.28%	>
Compare	Vanguard Australian Shares High Yield ETF ASX: VHY	ETF	0.25%	+12.17%	+10.46%	+7.85%	+9.13%	>
Compare	Vanguard Australian Shares High Yield Fund VAN0104AU	Managed fund	0.35%	+12.06%	+10.35%	+7.53%	+8.99%	>

I do not usually recommend the trading of shares directly, or foreign exchange, or CFDs (options). These are seen as a 'getting rich quick' secret formula. But there are so many advertisements on these topics. Most of those are from the platform company (market maker), who earn money from trading fees only. In contrast, a management fund usually earns a low management fee and profit share, so they have a vested interest in looking after your wealth.

I have seen many clients lose money on trading shares directly. Some platforms only give good examples, and make the users look like an expert, selling personal ego, giving away a lot of information to encourage people to trade frequently. In reality though, only a small number of people earn a lot of profit. For the rest, the profit is average and maybe not worth the time. Without the specific education and practice, a good mentor, system and tools, this is a demanding job by itself.

Below is another example from Vanguard Australian Shares Index ETF (2019), looking at the portfolio holdings. It is a demanding job to analyse so many companies, and doing your due diligence on all of them.

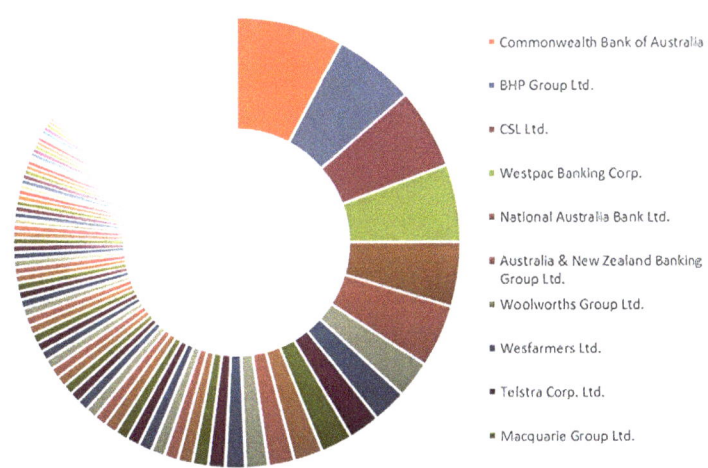

Holdings as at 30 September 2019 Data source: Vanguard Investments

4. **First Home Super Saver Scheme (Superannuation/FHSS Scheme):** You can only use this once and so need to use it wisely. But is the FHSS Scheme worth it? I would say yes, especially for people who earn more income than $45,000. Australia has a very high tax rate relative to other nations around the globe. This scheme offers you a once in a lifetime opportunity to pay less tax. It encourages you to park part of your income into your superannuation for the purpose of purchasing your first home. You can then withdraw it later to purchase your first home.

Rate	Current (2018 - 2022)	Proposed (2023 - 2024)
0%	0 - $18,200	0 - $18,200
19%	$18,200 - $37,000	$18,200 - **$45,000** [1]
32.5%	$37,001 - $90,000	**$45,001** - $120,000 [2]
37%	$90,001 - $180,000	$120,001 - $180,000
45%	$180,001 +	$180,001 +

(Source: Northern Business Consultants)

From the 1st of July 2022, there will be a couple of good changes for the First Home Buyer Super Saving Scheme. Firstly, the good news for everyone - the tax bracket drops the threshold. So, you pay less tax. Secondly, the maximum releasable amount increases from $30,000 to $50,000 towards the contribution. This means that you are paying less tax for an extra $20,000 salary sacrifice.

How To Save Faster Than Your Banks Want You To Know

You can visit Commonwealth Superannuation Corporation (www.csc.gov.au) and do the calculation and estimation yourself, to see how much extra this will help you to save.

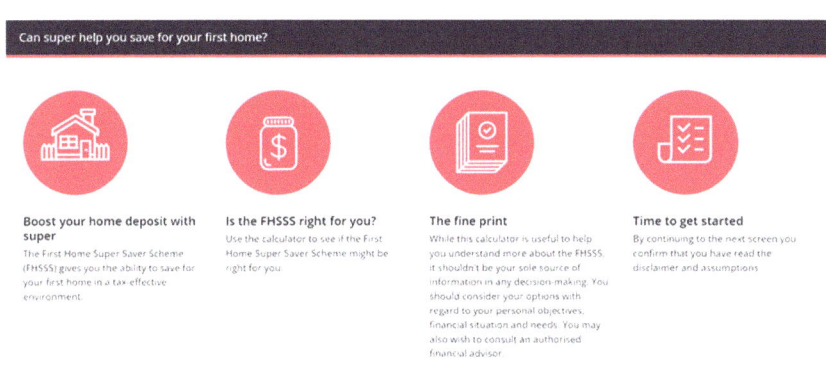

(Source: csc.gov.au)

Let's use two different income levels as example: $70,000 gross income per year plus super, and $120,000 gross income per year plus super. FHSS Scheme earns a deemed rate of interest set by the government (currently 3.04%, as of March 2022) rather than the full investment returns made by our superannuation. While lower than the typical 8% return on balanced funds, it's higher than interest rates on bank savings accounts. And, critically, it isn't affected by falling markets, which is especially important in this uncertain and volatile world, with factors such as COV-19 break out, new viruses, what is happening in Ukraine etc. to consider.

Retire On Rent

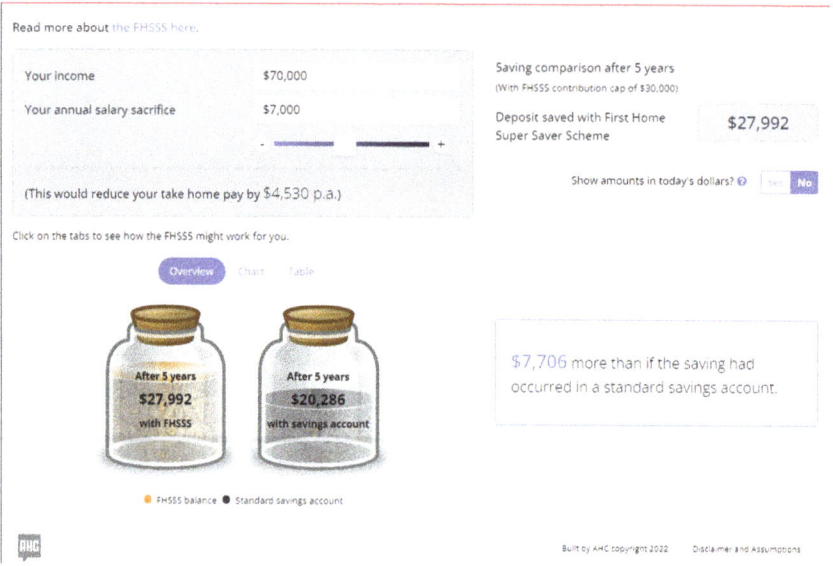

(Source: csc.gov.au)

This is an example of someone who is earning $70,000 a year and chooses to have a $7,000 salary sacrifice for the FHSS Scheme. The calculator shows he or she can save $7,706 extra compared to depositing into the normal savings account. Let's use this as a benchmark.

How To Save Faster Than Your Banks Want You To Know

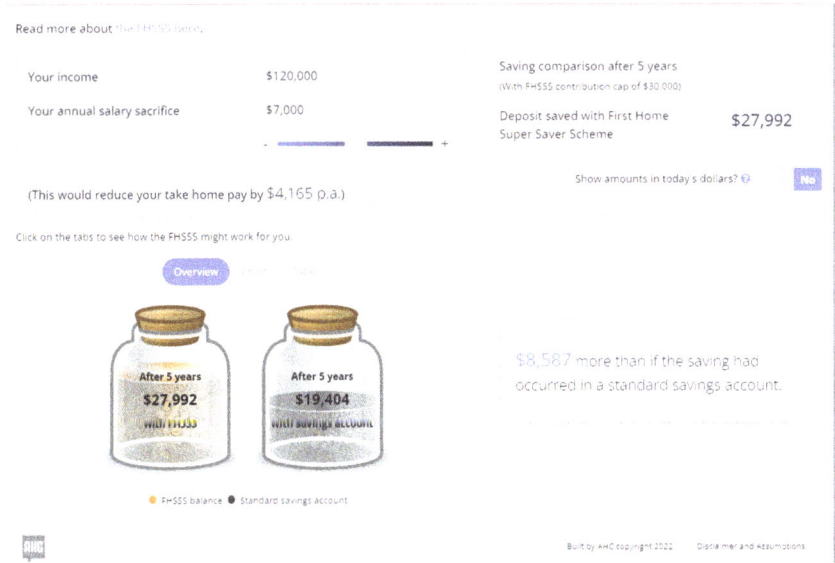

(Source: csc.gov.au)

Let's take the example of someone earning $120,000 and making the same contribution amount. You can see there is more saving in the bottom right of the above image - $8,587 compared to $7,706 in the previous example. It means a higher bracket can enjoy more tax savings.

*Disclaimer for the assumption - as of 2nd of March 2022, the example is based on the $30,000 cap for the FHSS Scheme and today's tax rate.

People do not have patience and long-term plans nowadays. Not many people plan two to five years ahead. They want every benefit now. If they cannot get it, some of them still do not plan ahead. Hence, this explains why the FHSS Scheme is less well known as First Home Deposit Scheme, and First

Home Buyer Scheme. A lot of people I meet, who did not get the quota for FHDS and FHBS, just give up rather than considering the FHSS Scheme. They go back to their old ways, spend a lot, save less, plan nothing.

5. Mortgage Fund: **Definition**: A type of investment fund where investors' money is on lent (as mortgage loans) to a range of borrowers who use the money to buy or develop properties. It might also be used for other investments (for example, investing in other mortgage funds). In return the fund manager promises to pay investors a regular income. [reference from SmartMoney.gov.au]

    Basically, you and a group of investors are lending money to a group of property investors or developers, via a mortgage fund manager. You are earning the interest return per project or per property, or pool of funds. The security is backed up by the property and its first mortgage right, so if the borrower defaults the loan, your mortgage manager will sell that property to take back the principle. Usually, the fund manager charges from 1% to 2% management fee and an establishment fee to the borrowers. So, for example, if the fund manager is lending money to a developer on a small building in Melbourne CBD worth $10 million dollars, and lends $5 mil to this developer for two years on an 8% interest rate, then the fund manager will pay the investors 6% interest return for whoever invests in this particular project. The developer may pay from 1% to 2% of the $5 mil loan amount once off to the fund manager to establish this debt facility as well.

How To Save Faster Than Your Banks Want You To Know

There are some examples in the market, as in the table below.

Risks and rewards from leading mortgage funds

Fund name & min investment ($)	Indicative returns pa* (%)	LVR**(%)	Investment terms
Alceon Debt Income Fund, 10,000	5.0-7.0	60-65	Min 12 mths
Australian Unity Select Income Fund, 5000	6.0-6.5	65	1-24 mths
La Trobe Australian Credit Fund, 10,000	5.0-5.5	60-65	Max 4 yrs for pooled fund; max 5 yrs for contributory fund
RMBL Mortgage Income Investments, 10,000	4.8-7.5	<67	1-3 yrs
Trilogy Monthly Income Trust, 10,000	5.15	63	Open-ended term
Balmain Discrete Mortgage Income Trust, 50,000	5.0-6.0	<65	6-18 mths
Equity-One Mortgage Fund, 10,000	5.0+	65-75	1 mth-5 yrs
Australian Securities Income Fund, 50,000	4.9	46	1-5 yrs

* Net of fees, includes pooled funds and contributory funds, see provider for details ** loan-to-value ratio

(Source: Australian Unity, Financial Review)

Although it sounds very safe and low risk, this method is not 'risk-free'. Over the years, I have seen people lose money on it. They invest in big or small fund providers. For first home buyers, or investors with lower risk appetite, it is wise to invest in the pool fund, with fixed term or fixed return, and it is not attached to any particular project or property. There are many options for the terms, from 30 days, 90 days, 180 days, one year, two years up to five years. Usually the longer the term, the higher the return is. However, usually I see one or two years as the most popular because it is easier to plan. Usually, the interest rate is payable monthly.

If you choose a pool of funds that invest in a range of different properties managed by the fund manager, your risk is exposed to a larger portfolio and the default risk offsetting each other. So even if one out of 100 properties go bust, you can still get your interest and principal back. If you invest in one particular project, usually you will get a few percent higher return, but if the project has any problems, you may delay getting your principal back, or worse, lose some money. If the project is land banking only, then it is usually lower risk. But if the project is involved with construction, then you are exposed to builder's risk as well.

The downside of a mortgage fund is no liquidation - usually you cannot break the term, or you can redeem the principal but with a penalty. For example, on a 5% annual return, if after half a year you want to withdraw, you need to pay a 2% penalty. So, your return for half a year is only 0.5%. With this in mind, people usually expect to commit for the whole term.

A few benchmarks to help you choose a good mortgage fund:

1. Reputation and track record: For Mum and Dad, or first home buyers, it is smart to avoid the fund that requires a minimum $500,000 investment as sophisticated investors, because they have higher risk, or are not tailored for small investors - they are not for beginners. Choose the one that only requires a couple of thousand dollars to start with, because they usually have a longer

tracking record, more disclosure of the portfolio, and with a better third-party rating agency.

2. Diversification and concentration risk by fund managers: It is better to avoid the fund manager that allocates more than 10% of their total funding to a particular project or developer group, or even builders. Otherwise, if that particular project, or developer, or builder goes bankrupt, the whole portfolio of the pool may lose 10% of its principal.

3. Do not chase the highest return: The higher the return, the higher the risk. We are already in the property investment segment, not Bitcoin, which should be steady and slow. Once a Jewish school mate in his sixth generation of family wealth shared with me one of their family investment principles: 'Be ready to lose your principal if the return is higher than 8%'. It is not saying do not invest in anything more than 8% return p.a., nor does it mean that below 8% is safer than 9%. It is simply a word of wisdom and experience, to do more homework if the return is higher than 8% as a benchmark. It is quite right in the mortgage fund investment industry.

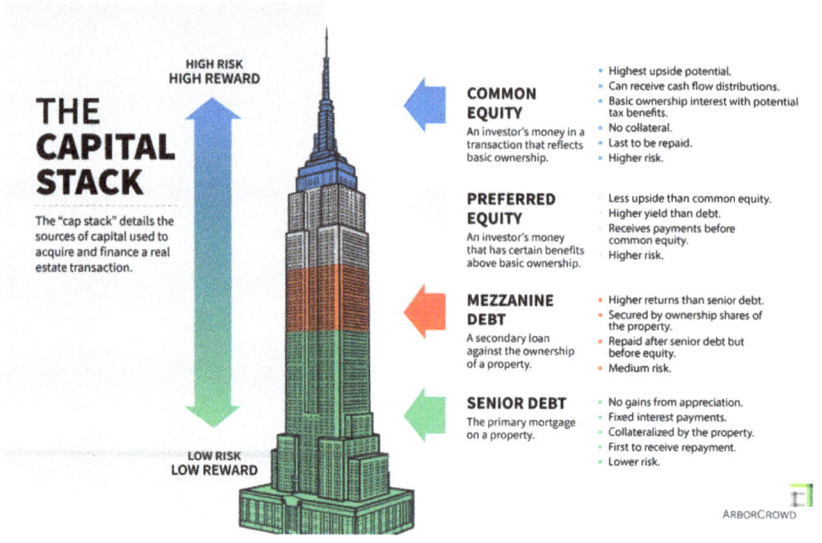

(source: www.arborcrowd.com)

There is a high return product in the mortgage funds, and they are riskier than a first mortgage. It usually occurs with mezzanine loans or second mortgages that are on top of the first mortgage or senior debt, on average delivering between 12% to 15% return. It often has the right to call the capital, i.e. to sell the security and take the principal back, in the event of borrowers' default to protect your principal. However, if it involves construction, or a high-risk project, both the senior debt and mezzanine debt may lose their principal all together.

4. Liquidation and redemption terms: Ask this question for all property funds, or even all investment types you want to invest in - 'What's the exit cost if I want to withdraw before the end of the term?' This is usually

defined in the redemption term in the funds. A lot of funds do not offer redemption at all. So, if you choose one or two or three years investment terms, you have to wait until the end of the term. Some of the funds allow redemption with 2% exit fee on average and require a 60-day early notice period.

Liquidation is very similar. This simply refers to how quickly you can sell it and get the money back. In the property fund market, unless you are investing in public listed property funds, or REITs (REITs, or real estate investment trusts, are companies that own or finance income-producing real estate), it is usually easier to resell within a few days, almost like the share market. There are always investors who want to replace your units.

5. LVR (Loan to Value Ratio): For example, for a $1 million property, you lend to the borrower 70%, which is $700,000, then the LVR is considered as 70%. The higher the LVR, the higher the risk. In the event of an economic downturn, the value of the property may decrease, the demand may decrease, and the number of buyers may decrease. If that happens, you may have to discount the house price in order to get the principal back quickly. This is also related to the concept of capital stacking above. Let's do a small exercise - which one of the two would you invest in?

Investment Options

(A) to invest in a property fund secured by a house in Toorak for $10 million, for a one-year loan term, the LVR is 50%, the return is 5% p.a.

(B) to invest in a property fund secured by a house in Toorak for $10 million, for a one-year loan term, the LVR is 70%, the return is 7% p.a.

There is no right or wrong answer - this is more about investors' risk tolerance.

6. Valuation risk: If you are investing in a particular project, usually it will disclose the valuation report by a third-party company. But there is a loophole in the system. Most investors do not have enough understanding of the valuation methodologies. The biggest risk to the investor is that they may think they lend the money to the borrower for 50% only. But 50% of what? Taking 'as if (future)' and 'as is (now)' as examples.

'As if' means the proposed value of the project if it is completed, i.e. with the assumption that all the 100 units of apartments that all have been sold and settled, or will be, the project is worth a lot of money. However, this project may still not even get the permit for 100 units yet. There are no legally effective pre-sales. There is a drawing of a 100 units apartment proposal yet to be lodged to the council. Let's say the project 'as if' value is $10 mil.

'As is' means the value is a piece of land at the moment, even if the permit is granted, but there are no pre-sales, there is no builder committed to start the construction yet - anything can still happen. The developer could change their mind and re-sell the land to another developer. The next developer may not like the previous permit and change it. In this circumstance, the land without the permit value is 'as is' value, which is only $3 million.

So, if you lend 50% LVR on 'as if' value of the above project, but really the project is not promising, you are actually lending on approximately 166% of the 'as is' value.

There are many unreputable valuation firms that produce reports for money.

Let me give you a recent live example, which happens almost every year. You can see my red highlight below; as conservative investors, you need to do more homework on investing in future 'artist impression' projects.

Retire On Rent

FINANCIAL REVIEW

Larry Schlesinger
Reporter

Feb 15, 2022 - 4.45pm

from private investors through a series of registered and unregistered managing investment schemes.

At its height, PE Capital claimed a $650 million pipeline of projects, including a 200-room Hyatt Hotel in the city's south-eastern suburbs that did not proceed.

Following proceeding lodged in May last year by the Australian Securities and Investments Commission, the Federal Court found that PE Capital breached the law by operating managed investment schemes without an Australian Financial Services licence and engaged in misleading and deceptive conduct.

"I am satisfied that it is in the public interest to wind up PE Capital Funds Management for the purpose of protecting investors and potential investors," Justice Cheeseman said.

An artist impression of the proposed Hyatt hotel in Springvale that was never built.

(Source: AFR, Federal Court judge orders winding up Melbourne Fund Manager PE Capital)

This is about discipline, not maths.

Definition of discipline by Google Dictionary: The practice of training people to obey rules or a code of behaviour, using punishment to correct disobedience.

Very often, it is not about choosing the best investment or saving products. Rather, it is about your behaviour, your commitment, your discipline. I have seen people set up joint investment accounts with their partner, or parents, and share half of the password with each other. That way, they cannot take money out without each other's consent. Alternatively they get two to sign, or joint signature.

How To Save Faster Than Your Banks Want You To Know

Some people do a regular salary sacrifice or split the salary into two accounts, one for daily living expenses, another one for minimum savings commitment to an investment or saving account that he or she cannot see and touch on their phone for a relatively long period of time.

What is the reward and the punishment? The reward is to print out the things you buy with it, i.e. your first or next home - put it on the wall or next to your savings jar. What is the punishment? Such as no dinner for a day, 20 push ups, or gardening. This could be a little homework for you - invite a friend or your partner to set up the gaming rules for your saving and investment game.

FOMO. The slower you save, the further distance you have to live from your friends and family (or the longer you have to live with your mum). Ultimately, it is all about saving up your deposit faster to buy your home. So, you do not have to pay $10,000 of LMI (Lending Mortgage Insurance, when you do not have enough savings for a first home), and you have the flexibility of not asking your parents to cash out from their home or provide parental guarantee.

FIRE - Financially Independent, Retire Early.

Another little secret is, the earlier you get into the property market, the earlier you can enjoy the property price increase. Usually, the property value increase will outperform most people's saving rate, and that is giving people a chance to refinance and take their equity out for the next property investment deposit. FOMO, again.

CHAPTER FOUR

THE RISKS OF INVESTING IN PROPERTIES – KNOW THEM BEFORE YOU BUY THEM

Most investors only see the benefits of investing in property, but are not as well-prepared or knowledgeable when it comes to the risk of property investment. The reality is, I have seen many investors lose money and gain unnecessary stress when entering into property investment. All this can be avoided, if you see both sides and have a clear picture of risks associated. Once my mentor told me, 'The real risks are the things you neglect and remain unknown due to your lack of knowledge, being arrogant, overconfident, and unprepared. But risks are not the ones that you foresee, and you must have mitigation measurements in place.'

Retire On Rent

Ancient Chinese translated the word 'Crisis' as 'Wei-Ji'; it means 'dangerous and opportunities'. It tells us that there is profit in every change. Do not be afraid of the risks, acknowledge and embrace them. Risk is not necessarily bad. Prepare with your own strategies to cope with the changes along the way.

Check out the statistics, you can Google them yourself. I do it every year as a hobby: 'people who own more than two properties in Australia' or 'investors with more than five investment properties' - there will be many interesting articles with statistics and reports appearing.

It is important to think for yourself, do your research and start your property portfolio with a clear vision. Below is an interesting view of the property investor demographic.

HOW MANY INVEST?

%	
91.53%	No investment property - 22.8 million people
7.65%	1-2 properties - 1.9 million people
0.49%	3 properties - 122,500 people
0.33%	4 or more properties - 82,500 people

- 91.5% of Australian's do not invest in property
- 9/10 Australian property investors fail to build their portfolio past 1 or 2 properties

Source: ATO Tax Stats April 2017

The Risks Of Investing In Properties

The Australian Taxation Office recently released their latest stats on property investment, so let's see how rich property investors really are.

Here is a quick summary…

According to CoreLogic:

- There are 10.5 million dwellings in Australia with a total value of $7.1 trillion
- There is a total of $1.85 trillion in outstanding mortgage debt
- 52.5% of Australian household wealth is held in housing

The Australian Taxation Office tells us that in the 2017-18 tax year (the latest statistics available):

- There are 2,207,893 property investors in Australia
- This means around 20% of Australian households hold an investment property and 80% don't.
- The top investor age groups are:
    - 27.83% are aged 60 or more
    - 31.67% are aged between 50 and 59 years
    - 24.65% are aged between 40 and 49 years
    - 14.22% are aged between 30 and 39 years
    - Just 1.63% are younger than 30.
- Here's how many properties investors hold
    - 1 investment property - 71% (1.57 million) - increased by 2.3% over the last year
    - 2 investment properties - 19% (418,000) - increased by 2.7% over the last year

- 3 investment properties - 6% (129,784) - increased by 3% over the last year
- 4 investment properties - 2% (47,469) - increased by 2.2% over the last year
- 5 investment properties - 1% (19,861) - increased by 1.8% over the last year
- 6 or more investment properties - less than 1% (20,756) – increased by 2% in the last year

How much are these property investors earning?

Nothing much has changed over the years. Hence why I want to emphasise the importance of financial literacy and research. The fact that 90% of investors only own one or two investment properties has been the status quo for many years.

● 30.4%
Difficulty with loan serviceability
547 responses

● 14.5%
Not having enough deposit or equity
262 responses

● 24%
Uncertainty about the economy or the future of our property markets
433 responses

● 7.7%
Other
138 responses

● 3.9%
Negative cash flow
70 responses

● 19.5%
I don't have a major obstacle
352 responses

The Risks Of Investing In Properties

Note: The 2018 Property Investor Sentiment Survey was conducted by *Michael Yardney's Property Update*.

Now, let's discuss it thoroughly. Here are the risk factors plus my recommendation for the mitigations. There are many different risks you can look up on Google. Again, this book is better than Google - it is a comprehensive guideline, provided by someone who has done it before and continues doing it daily for many clients. Also, this book is aiming to provide you constructive solutions, as opposed to some online blog articles that only tell you part of, or a small piece of information.

Category	Risk Factors
External Influence	Natural disaster
	Market risk
	Government policies change
	Bank policies change
	Bank mortgage rates increasing
Risks Related to Properties	Inherent property quality risk
	Maintenance cost
	High vacancy rate
	Tenancy profile risk
	You invest in the wrong property types
	You invest in the wrong suburbs
	You buy at the wrong time
	You sell at the wrong time
	Construction risk
	Property price goes down

Category	Risk Factors
Self-imposed Risks	High level of entry, especially on equity, saving and borrowing power
	High holding costs such as increasing interest rate and tax
	Lack of investment strategies
	Lack of investment knowledge
	Over-committed
	Financially unprepared
	Emotionally unprepared
	Credit risk
	Refinance risk
	Investors lose the job

Taking these into account, I want to raise a question: who do you think will teach you all these factors?

You will not be able to get all of this information from one particular person; it is through different professionals. But the problem with all the professionals is they are busy and less proactive. This is not their forte. Let's face it, most of them do not have the time to even sell courses. And, on the other hand, I have found that many people who sell courses are not professionals themselves. They are just good at talking and marketing without much substance. All they want to sell is their own products, such as properties or more expensive courses later on.

Of course, there is nothing wrong with all that because I went through many of them. A few of the courses were very worthwhile. However, what I want to emphasise here is that it's your own responsibility as a long-term property investor to be aware of all the associated risks, and be responsible for your own decisions. The more knowledge you have, the more successful you will be. I have another chapter further on which will explain how to utilise different professionals in property investment.

First of all, as a long-term investor, every time you see risk, you should feel excited. I know this is a foreign concept but believe me, it works. You have to learn to be friends with risks, understand them, say hi to them, acknowledge that they are there. Learn about them, their pattern, how other people usually react to them, what is the cause of them, when they come and go. Once you become friends with them, whilst other people are afraid of them, you then win in the investment game. The better you know them, the more you can master the profit.

Here are some of my recommendations for risk mitigation you could consider:

<u>No.1: Read widely about economics, including famous books, video, and the news, to be familiar with the economic cycle.</u>
I would start by recommending you watch the YouTube Video 'How the Economic Machine Works' by Ray Dalio, one of the legends in share market investment. This 31-minute animated video is the best I have seen that explains how the economic cycle works and how the banks manage the mortgage rate fluctuation. Once you understand the pattern of the economic

cycle which comes and goes every seven to ten years, you sort of learn the expectation of what you will go through during each economic cycle and feel more comfortable and calm about it. I have to say I fell asleep in my uni economics lecture, but I watched this video multiple times because it is so fun to learn.

I do not want to reinvent the wheel, and for that reason it is important to refer to other content in my book that might be helpful. I just want to help you to set up a structural thinking framework that will help you to navigate the world of property investment.

<u>No.2: Gather the facts and statistics for the capital city and suburbs you want to invest in.</u>
There are so many free and affordable property reports out there but let's take a look at some examples of basic data.

1. Population growth: The faster the population growth in the local city council or suburbs nearby, the more it will drive up the demand of the house price. A good example is Sydney and Melbourne, who have the largest population growth and also enjoy the fastest and long-term house price growth.

    In recent years, due to COVID changing people's lifestyles, the Tasmanian government began providing permanent residency for young people with skills who want to move there, thus raising the property price. There is also big growth overall in Brisbane and Hobart. If you dig into the recent sales price history via RealEstate.

The Risks Of Investing In Properties

com.au, you will be amazed by how much the house prices are going up and the level of buyers' interest.

The best website to go to for free for local suburb population, income profile and many other important facts is the Australian Bureau of Statistics (https://www.abs.gov.au/). I love this website; it is like the weather but forecasting the Australian economy.

BRISBANE: Up 30.4% to $782,967
SYDNEY: Up 29.6% to $1,374,970
CANBERRA: Up 27.2% to $1,015,900
HOBART: Up 26.7% to $747,187
ADELAIDE: Up 25.8% to $622,155
MELBOURNE: Up 17.9% to $997,928
PERTH: Up 13.3% to $553,013
DARWIN: Up 12.4% to $565,080

Source: CoreLogic data on median house prices annual increases in December 2021

2. Average income per household: Think of this, if you are investing in a suburb where the average house price is below the median house price in that capital city, but the household income is higher than the median or average income, then you immediately see a growth opportunity. Or you can also relate to people's income and the kind of property they will buy. Their ability to increase their income is also one of the drivers for future house price.

A simple example is Clayton and Clayton South in Victoria, where Monash University has its biggest campus. It is one of the lowest tax collection suburbs, because the majority of the local residents are students. Property investors love to buy properties to rent to students. And they love to develop student accommodation, rooming houses and multi-unit townhouses, for higher rent yield. However, the house price goes up very slowly in Clayton. And when COV-19 came in 2020 and 2021, we lost most of the international students, and local students' study at home, so house prices crashed in Clayton. There is a little typhoon here but not many people notice. Just like another CBD in Melbourne. At the end of the day, as a landlord, you do not just want to collect the rent, you also want to sell the house one day to someone who can afford it and ideally this purchaser will rent in this or the surrounding suburbs for a long time. You can increase the rent with less competitors in the area.

3. Age and demography: A suburb with an aging demographic but a young population coming in is a growing suburb for ten years. For example, in Frankston and Frankston South in Victoria, the elderly have been downsizing and moving to smaller units, apartments, or residential care facilities. At the same time, more and more people from other suburbs in Victoria or interstate, or even new immigrants, are moving down here for houses or newly built townhouses for family. There is more childcare as well. So, new childcare or

full childcare centres are also indicators of the local demographics as well.

4. Local economic drivers and activities: What do the people do in the local suburbs? Are they doing a variety of different jobs? Or do most of them rely on one single company, such as Holden in Geelong; when the Geelong factory closed, the house prices in the surrounding suburbs decreased for a couple of years, and then moved back up for many other reasons. Or, if the local suburbs are relying on a mining company, or a military base, or a big ship factory, or farming industry - is that industry on an incline or decline? Are they stable? What's their status in the economic cycle? Personally, I would prefer to invest somewhere with a more diversified economy, and I prefer not to invest in a mining town with high rental or high property price, unless the government has a plan to develop that area into a metropole city or satellite city.

The reason for this is simple. House price growth is based on consistent population growth for the foreseeable generations. If a company or an industry leaves those local suburbs, or is relocated, it takes the labour and economy with it. It will be a ghost town where prices are bound to decrease, and even worse, there is no enquiry to buy. What if you are planning to sell a property for your retirement or estate planning? And suddenly your asset is worthless?

I have seen that happen. In Western Australia for example, in recent years due to the mining industry downturn and a bad relationship with China, the house price decreased significantly, people could not refinance, and some people sold their properties at a loss.

5. Proportion of owner occupiers and investors: Ideally you want to invest in a suburb or a multi-unit residential development (such as 20 townhouses in a few rows), which is mostly owner-occupied. Owner occupiers are still the main driver of property price increase. They are the emotional buyers who are willing to spend their biggest savings on your investment property when you are trying to sell it. For example, if you invested in an apartment in Docklands, Victoria, or a townhouse in Clayton, where the international students are not coming back, half of the apartments buildings or the suburbs are empty. This makes the rent yield very low, vacancy very long, and selling price hard to cover your costs. The ABS and even Core Logic Report will give you a lot of information on this to make a more informed purchase.

6. Transport: This includes highway, public transport, normal roads - simply how easy it is for the residents to commute. You will find that a suburb on the train line usually has higher prices than one off the train line. If a resident is in a remote area, the price will be significantly lower.

The Risks Of Investing In Properties

7. Schools: Proximity to schools really will help to maintain the value of house prices or even drive them much harder, whether they are private or public schools. Of course, the good public schools are more desirable because you have to live in a particular zone, also by renting, to get into the catchment of the area. This includes both primary and secondary schools. Here is the Domain School Zone Report 2021.

PRIMARY SCHOOLS | SECONDARY SCHOOLS

Search top primary schools | Embed

#	SCHOOL NAME	STATE	MEDIAN	YOY	
1	Burraneer Bay Public School	NSW	$2,100,000	44.8% ▲	View Catchments
2	Newport Public School	NSW	$2,675,000	43.0% ▲	View Catchments
3	West End State School	QLD	$1,325,000	41.7% ▲	View Catchments
4	Woy Woy Public School	NSW	$870,000	41.5% ▲	View Catchments
5	Richmond Primary School	VIC	$1,842,500	39.6% ▲	View Catchments
6	Kimberley Park State School	QLD	$620,000	38.2% ▲	View Catchments
7	Kellyville Ridge Public School	NSW	$1,377,500	37.8% ▲	View Catchments
8	Harbord Public School	NSW	$3,050,000	37.6% ▲	View Catchments
9	Kincumber Public School	NSW	$912,500	36.9% ▲	View Catchments
10	Heidelberg Primary School	VIC	$1,510,000	36.7% ▲	View Catchments

Retire On Rent

	SCHOOL NAME	STATE	MEDIAN	YOY	
1	Barrenjoey High School	NSW	$2,802,500	45.0% ▲	View Catchments
2	Eastern Hills Senior High School	WA	$602,500	41.8% ▲	View Catchments
3	Cronulla High School	NSW	$2,030,000	40.0% ▲	View Catchments
4	Kiara College	WA	$417,500	39.2% ▲	View Catchments
5	Kogarah High School	NSW	$1,300,000	38.4% ▲	View Catchments
6	Kincumber High School	NSW	$1,175,000	38.2% ▲	View Catchments
7	Woolooware High School	NSW	$1,610,000	34.2% ▲	View Catchments
8	Mosman High School	NSW	$4,000,000	33.3% ▲	View Catchments
9	Diamond Valley College	VIC	$990,000	33.2% ▲	View Catchments
10	Bayview Secondary College	TAS	$447,500	32.6% ▲	View Catchments

Reference: https://www.domain.com.au/research/school-zones-report/2021/

It is worthwhile studying the local school rankings, and its criteria. People tend to invest or spend a lot of money on their children's education without budgeting. They love their children and give all they can. I used to take an Uber and the driver was a father who drove as a second job, driving an Uber at night to pay for his children's private school fees. He went out of his way.

You can always learn. Me personally, I used to want to buy property in Diamond Valley as an investment.

The Risks Of Investing In Properties

That was in 2015, and now I feel such regret since looking up this property report.

8. Amenities, local shopping, and lifestyle: This is what is being referred to in the saying, 'Location, location, location'. The parks, the library, the community centre, the shopping centre - all this will add value to the convenience of living. People are more willing to pay higher prices or rent for a lifestyle.

    Some people will use McDonalds, KFC, Coles, or other big retail brands as the radar when they invest in property.

9. Average local property prices and data: You need to do the analysis about the local property price, such as the recent transaction prices, average and medium price point, rental yield and vacancy rate.

    This is important for your strategy setting. Are you going to buy a good house in a cheap suburb, or a cheap house in a good suburb? There is no wrong or right, but you need to know your position.

10. Upcoming development sites: A lot of this data is available online, on official council websites, or local newspapers. Or, you can even drive around an area. More townhouses being built is actually a good sign, it simply means more and more residents want to live in this suburb, but the land price is high so people may not afford a big house. Instead, they choose to

move into the townhouses. Some areas will have new shopping centres, new childcare facilities, new school zone expansions. For example, McKinnon Secondary School in Victoria expanded its school zone and built a new campus which immediately drove up the land price in the Bentleigh area. Personally, I have an investment property in Bentleigh East, outside the McKinnon School Zone. My friend purchased a property in Bentleigh East, two minutes away. Her house was not in the McKinnon School Zone initially, but luckily, it was included in the new school zone. We both did a bank valuation on our property in 2018 before COV-19 and late 2021 after COV-19. My bank valuation increased by $200,000, and her house increased by $400,000, double my value. The discussion of where the new school zone may be has been going on for a few years. Clearly, it is worthwhile to be a local suburb expert.

11. Unique natural beauty location profile: Coastline is one of the best examples of this, as are national parks, hot springs, big farms, tourism attractions. Actually, a lot of these cannot be found in many reports. The best way to find out about them is to drive around the local suburbs.

12. Crime statistics: You can simply look these up online via ABS or look up 'latest crime data by area' on the government website (for example: https://www.crimestatistics.vic.gov.au/). This can be complicated - some investors really care about who their potential

tenants are, and potential experience. If there is higher crime rate, it may mean lower rent growth or capital growth. There are many different categories of crime, such as drugs, burglary, domestic violence. Also, there are different reasons for it - is it because of local demographic profile, low-income social status, low education level?

For me, personally, crime statistics have not affected my investment considerations. An example of this is Frankston, again in Victoria. Despite being known for having a high crime rate, house prices and rental prices still go up very steadily. A few more examples are, also in Victoria, suburbs known for being drug area and having gangs, such as Springvale, Sunshine, even Box Hill years ago, which are all now expensive suburbs in Melbourne. So personally, I recommend being aware of the local crime statistics, but not basing your investment decision solely on them.

An index is provided for property data and report helping you to make more informative decision.

No.3: Visit somewhere physically yourself, have a coffee there

As discussed above, it is very difficult to read the cold data and try to understand a local suburb and its potential. If allowed, it is best to drive around the local area, have a coffee, to get a feeling about it. Ask friends who may live there, speak to the local shop owners, hear what they say about their areas.

If you are looking at the cars in the car park outside Woolworth or Coles, you may do an income and expenses analysis for the local residents.

No.4: Choose the right property type and budget

This may be contradictory to your normal thinking that 'apartments are always bad for investment; land is always good'. It is more important to choose the right property type, at the right price range, in the right suburbs. The principle is, choosing the one for which there is more demand but less supply.

Consider Point Cook in Victoria, where house and land package were over-supplied for a long period of time. People could always find a new house and land package in Point Cook; hence the second-hand property price has grown slowly. There are not enough schools or shopping areas yet in the early stages of the suburb development. On the other hand, there are some low-density beachline apartments whose prices are rising faster than some houses.

There is not one type that fits all. Think in different contexts and from different perspectives.

> **Dialectical reasoning** is the process of arriving at truth through a process of comparing and contrasting various solutions. This process, also known as logic, originated in classical Greece by the philosopher Aristotle and has evolved into the present through the works of other philosophers such as Hegel.

The Risks Of Investing In Properties

<u>No.5: Do a ten-year forecast and budgeting with multiple up and down factors in your assumption (best scenario and worst scenario)</u>

This does not have to be fancy, but you have to consider the ups and downs and as many factors as possible. Some agencies will only tell you about the good part - the capital growth and rental growth. But other people only tell you the bad parts to scare you.

I have just spent five minutes on the below spreadsheet, making very conservative assumptions, such as including vacancy rate, putting on high maintenance budget, and a high mortgage rate at 5.5% on average for the next ten years. Do not be scared by the negative cashflow, as it may be positive after tax with the depreciation or negative gearing. Ask your accountant now how much you may earn if you sell it at the end of ten years. Do not ask them ten years later, like most people do.

Retire On Rent

10 Years Cashflow Forecast

Assumption	
Capital Growth Per Year	7.20%
Average Mortgage Rate	5.50%
Rental Growth	3%
Rental Income Per Week	$ 450.00
Vacancy Rate	1.5 weeks

	Year 1	Year 2	Year 3	Year 4	Year 5	Year 6	Year 7	Year 8	Year 9	Year 10	Year 11
House Price	$700,000	$750,400	$804,429	$862,348	$924,437	$990,996	$1,062,348	$1,138,837	$1,220,833	$1,308,733	$1,402,962
Loan Amout	$560,000	(if you pay principle, or utilize offset account, this will decrease year by year)									
Loan: If Interest Only All Time	$30,800	$30,800	$30,800	$30,800	$30,800	$30,800	$30,800	$30,800	$30,800	$30,800	$30,800
Loan: If P & I All Time	$38,160	$38,160	$38,160	$38,160	$38,160	$38,160	$38,160	$38,160	$38,160	$38,160	$38,160
Assume All Other Maintainance Cost	$2,000	$2,000	$2,000	$2,000	$2,000	$2,000	$2,000	$2,000	$2,000	$2,000	$2,000
Rental Income Per Year (minus 1.5 weeks vacancy)	$22,725	$23,407	$24,109	$24,832	$25,577	$26,345	$27,135	$27,949	$28,787	$29,651	$30,540
Strategy 1 Before Tax Cashflow (if I.O. all time)	($10,075)	($9,393)	($8,691)	($7,968)	($7,223)	($6,455)	($5,665)	($4,851)	($4,013)	($3,149)	($2,260)
Cashflow in Weeks out of pocket	($194)	($181)	($167)	($153)	($139)	($124)	($109)	($93)	($77)	($61)	($43)
Strategy 2 Before Tax Cashflow (if P & I all time)	($17,435)	($16,753)	($16,051)	($15,328)	($14,583)	($13,815)	($13,025)	($12,211)	($11,373)	($10,509)	($9,620)
Cashflow in Weeks out of pocket	($335)	($322)	($309)	($295)	($280)	($266)	($250)	($235)	($219)	($202)	($185)
After Tax Cashflow											
Depreciation Benefit	Each individual circumstance and each house are different.										
Negative Gearing or Accumulated Loss											

It is best to err on the side of caution when calculating your cash flow interest. You need to face the worst-case scenario and still confidently having the strategies to cope with the low period before you can enjoy the capital growth.

The Risks Of Investing In Properties

10 Years Cashflow Forecast

Assumption		
Capital Growth Per Year	7.20%	
Average Mortgage Rate	3.50%	
Rental Growth	3%	
Rental Income Per Week	$ 450.00	
Vacancy Rate	1.5 weeks	

	Year 1	Year 2	Year 3	Year 4	Year 5	Year 6	Year 7	Year 8	Year 9	Year 10	Year 11
House Price	$700,000	$750,400	$804,429	$862,348	$924,437	$990,996	$1,062,348	$1,138,837	$1,220,833	$1,308,733	$1,402,962
Loan Amout	$560,000	(if you pay principle, or utilize offset account, this will decrease year by year)									
Loan: If Interest Only All Time	$19,600	$19,600	$19,600	$19,600	$19,600	$19,600	$19,600	$19,600	$19,600	$19,600	$19,600
Loan: If P & I All Time	$38,160	$38,160	$38,160	$38,160	$38,160	$38,160	$38,160	$38,160	$38,160	$38,160	$38,160
Assume All Other Maintainance Cost	$2,000	$2,000	$2,000	$2,000	$2,000	$2,000	$2,000	$2,000	$2,000	$2,000	$2,000
Rental Income Per Year (minus 1.5 weeks vacancy)	$22,725	$23,407	$24,109	$24,832	$25,577	$26,345	$27,135	$27,949	$28,787	$29,651	$30,540
Strategy 1 Before Tax Cashflow (If I.O. all time)	$1,125	$1,807	$2,509	$3,232	$3,977	$4,745	$5,535	$6,349	$7,187	$8,051	$8,940
Cashflow in Weeks out of pocket											
After Tax Cashflow						Each individual circumstance and each house are different.					
Depreciation Benefit											
Negative Gearing or Accumulated Loss											

My question to you is, assuming you are going to sell your property in Year 3, Year 5 or Year 11, at different market condition, would you still make a profit? Bear in mind all the set-up costs, such as stamp duty, and selling costs, such as capital gains tax.

No.6: The cheapest insurance is the most expensive insurance

I have seen many landlords trying to claim insurance with little success. To be honest, most people buy insurance to satisfy banking settlement requirements, and never ask what is being covered, or terms and conditions to claim. Very often, people tend to choose the cheapest insurance, just by comparing prices. You get what you pay for. Imagine if you pay insurance for $500 per year, instead of $800 per year. After ten years, you've paid $5,000, you want to make an $80,000 lost claim for house damage, and you get nothing because it is not covered, or you do not meet the requirements. Compare this with having paid $800 for ten years which is $8,000, but you get covered for $80,000.

Which one is more expensive?

No.7: Appoint the right professional

By now, you may be dizzy from trying to absorb all of this information. This has taken me ten years to learn and I am still learning. And I am still not qualified or confident enough to give you tax advice, or legal advice. As a very senior mortgage broker, I still ask my colleagues in my mortgage broker firm or other firms many questions about recent mortgage policy updates.

Surround yourself with the true experts so you can focus on your daily job and enjoy your living, even with some costs. I will have another chapter about how to select and differentiate the professionals.

The Risks Of Investing In Properties

No.8: Find the right classmates and seek peer support

People are naturally lazy as human beings, including myself. We always make excuses and find reasons not to get something done, or even make a start. Property investment and personal finance are really about discipline. You do not have to be a genius or good at maths. Property investment is one of the simplest and safest investment options in Australia. You have to read the news regularly, look up the suburbs regularly, visit the sites, and learn consistently.

Find your 'investment comrade'. Find a group of people who share the same goals and are committed to them. Maintain communication with your peer group, share information, and encourage each other. Learn from each other's mistakes, and encourage a sharing culture. When you see one of your 'comrade's' success, it will encourage you to take more action and believe that it is doable and possible. 'If she or he can do it, I can do it too.'

No. 9: Stay away from multiple unit constructions for beginners

It is my passion and bread and butter to finance multiple units and I do it myself to escalate my rental book accumulation. However, I have also paid a big price for this, losing money, facing uncertainly and pressure. This is definitely not for beginners. And it requires a lot more capital, income servicing, time committed to learn, and willingness to fail.

I also help a lot of developers and builders with their finance - many people actually lose significant amount money or even go bankrupt.

You do not have to be a developer to get financial freedom or 'retire with rent'.

<u>No.10: Enjoy what you do</u>
My final point is a simple one – enjoy what it is that you're doing!

CHAPTER FIVE

HOLDING COSTS FOR AN INVESTMENT PROPERTY IN AUSTRALIA – SECRETS THE AGENTS WILL NEVER TELL YOU

I'm going to let you in on a secret – not everyone is on your side so you must make sure you do your own research when it comes to your precious finances and investments.

For instance, there's a little thing called "holding costs" that are often the undoing of property investors. So, what is a holding cost?

Holding cost is all the associated expense when you own a property from the date of a new settlement until the date of selling.

And you should never underestimate it.

Not many properties investment books in Australia will actually talk about the additional expenses from holding costs when investing in a property, nor the risk of investing in it. Whether the agents know or don't know about it, it must be a definite consideration when investing in property.

So as a property portfolio owner, you need to go into the investment with your eyes open, to see if buying 'this' investment property will still be as profitable as you think.

'Do your research!' is a must but be careful where you get your information. Once again, not all is as it seems. Take the issue of the Google search engine; nowadays it is all about the Google Ads fees and SEO (Search Engine Optimisation); whoever pays for the ads and SEO fees will show up on the first page. This is why people see marketing gurus rather than subject matter online. Think of it this way; do you go to a doctor when you are sick or Google how to fix it yourself?

As for literature on the subject, unfortunately most books and promoted investment articles are trying to sell you a particular type of investment property; how to hold it, why you should buy it, and not many outline the details of the cost items and potential risks. So, I will use two chapters to illustrate these two important elements in property investment – costs and risks.

It's a hard fact to swallow but most people in investments do not get to see the profit. Of course, there are vendor agents and buyer agents in the market, but all of these

Holding Costs For An Investment Property In Australia

come with expenses and are not necessarily looking after the purchaser's interest. A vendor agent's job is to sell the property for the vendor, so that they do not have to educate you about additional costs and risks. And the buyer agents will charge you 2%, or $15,000 to $20,000 minimum, to tell you this. And there are 'marketing agents' packaging themselves as 'property advisors', charging the purchaser a $3,000 to $6,000 'course fee' and selling them off-the-plan townhouses or house and land packages, while getting paid by the developer $20,000 per unit that they sell. The course fee makes the 'investor' feel like they did the research. A large part of the course content, I agree, is helpful, but each of us needs to be aware and cool down, to consider if that product is really for you. There might be nothing wrong with it, but it is not for everyone.

As you can see, you could have just saved yourself $20,000 by reading this chapter.

I would also like to make it clear, there is no license or no degree for a 'property advisor' course. It is a job title, not a professional title. There is no such qualification, you cannot find any university course, it is only experience that gives someone this title. There is a two-week Real Estate Agents Course Certificate IV, and two-week Mortgage Broker Course Certificate IV, to manage most family's most important assets. But what you need to be mindful of is how people earn the money from you. What do they disclose, and is that in alignment with your long-term best interest? Are they sharing the risks with you? There is no professional indemnity insurance to cover the so-called property advisor's mistakes, not like lawyers, doctors, accountants, financial planners. For those who don't know, the definition of professional indemnity insurance is as follows: Professional indemnity insurance covers the cost of compensating clients for loss or damage resulting from negligent services or advice provided by a business or an individual.

There are three categories of costs associated with buying a property as your investment property:

A. The costs associated with buying an investment property.
B. The costs associated with holding the property every year.
C. The costs of selling a property.

So, the maths is simple. Selling price – all costs (incl. tax) = your profit in the end for your retirement. Or you can turn the property into a positive cashflow (after tax) as your cash cow and hold it until you go into heaven (Estate Planning is another topic for another day - how to hold properties through generation after generation).

Now, let's break it down.

Holding Costs For An Investment Property In Australia

Part A: Costs of purchasing an investment property at settlement

A.1. Stamp duty 3% to 5.5%

This is the once-off tax charged by the State Revenue Office (SRO) according to the property contract price. If you are a foreign passport owner (not Australia and New Zealand), you will also need to pay an extra 8% of the property price as foreign tax.

There is also one-off Land Transfer Fee and Mortgage Title Registration Fee charged by the government at settlement.

Stamp duty paid in different states and territories will vary, though most tend to charge similar amounts. On a **$500,000** property, the stamp duty payable per state (as per January 2022) is:

State	Stamp Duty	Transfer Fee	Mortgage Registration Fee	Total
ACT	$ 10,360.00	$ 416.00	$ 155.00	$ 10,931.00
VIC	$ 21,970.00	$ 1,261.00	$ 112.40	$ 23,343.40
NSW	$ 17,707.00	$ 147.70	$ 147.70	$ 18,002.40
QLD	$ 8,750.00	$ 1,381.00	$ 197.00	$ 10,328.00
SA	$ 21,330.00	$ 4,330.50	$ 176.00	$ 25,836.50
TAS	$ 18,247.50	$ 216.15	$ 141.07	$ 18,604.72
NT	$ 23,928.60	$ 152.00	$ 152.00	$ 24,232.60
WA	$ 17,765.00	$ 271.30	$ 181.30	$ 18,217.60

Stamp Duty paid in different states on a $500,000 property (as per January 2022)

For more specific numbers, you can look up SRO website in the state you are purchasing and put it in your budget.

Property buyers are required to pay stamp duty costs up front, i.e. when the transaction is finalised, and contracts are exchanged. The exact time frame varies across states and territories. We've summarised the payable time frames in each state and territory below.

NSW – payable within three months of settlement
ACT – payable within 28 days of settlement
VIC – payable within 30 days of the property being transferred
QLD – payable within 30 days of settlement
SA – payable on settlement day
WA – payable within two months of settlement
NT – payable within 60 days of entering into the transaction or at settlement, whichever is earlier
TAS – payable within three months of a transfer occurring.

Some investors prefer house and land packages because they only pay stamp duty on the land contract price, not the building contract price. For example, if the land price is $300,000 plus a build contract of $300,000, then the investor is technically paying half of the stamp duty.

A.2. Minimum deposit – Recommend from 20%
I am a very conservative investor, so I would usually recommend to prepare for 20% minimum saving plus all other government costs, and legal costs, to purchase a property.

However, sometimes it is wise to pay Lending Mortgage Insurance (LMI). It depends on your personal circumstances. You may want to buy time for the future, rather than waiting to save up the 20%, and then get into the market earlier, otherwise the house price may increase by the time you have the 20%. Some banks offer minimum 5% to 10% deposit plus government costs, and other costs associated, plus a LMI costs roughly 2%.

Holding Costs For An Investment Property In Australia

*LMI is a concept is explained in more detail below in A.6. cost item.

However, if you are investing in commercial real estate, the deposit will require more, such as a 30% to 40% deposit.

A.3. Legal and conveyancing – recommend at $2,200:
There is no set market price on legal fees. It is a professional service, so each firm may charge differently and in different states. In Victoria for example, the average conveyancing fee is between $800 and $1,200 plus GST. For more complicated properties, you may need to pay more. If the lawyer read the contract and you did not end up buying, the lawyer may charge $200 plus GST per contract reading. So usually, I will leave $2,000 legal fee in my own budgeting.

My advice is to try to find a reputable legal firm with comprehensive legal services, including real estate, estate planning, commercial and business law, etc. You can save money on banks and interest rates, but never on professional services like lawyers and accountants.

A.4. Bank fees – recommend at $660:
The bank may charge a $395 annual fee to waive the $10 to $15 monthly fee, and waive the $600 settlement fee, and waive the valuation fee around $300 to $500. Annual packages will provide an offset account, which gives the investors tax advantages and more flexibility.

If there is no annual fee, then the above fee is usually required. So usually, I will include a $600 budget at the settlement, and

$395 annually. Personally, I prefer the package product with an annual fee, which drives on average a lower rate over a longer term of the loan. You save the money back in the end. The base loan may not have an ongoing annual fee, but after the honeymoon period (6-24 months), I personally observe that the base loan rate is no different to the package loan rate, or sometimes higher. But base loan does not have the flexibility for ongoing maintenance, such as splitting the loan in a mix of fixed and variable loan. I will explain this in more detail in another chapter about the loan products.

The discharge cost can also not be neglected when you are selling your property or refinancing, which is the same discharge cost. Usually it is $350, plus a title deregister fee by the government.

A.5. Property inspection cost – recommend at $550
It's vital to invest in a good quality property and maintain it well. So, property inspection, at least for me, is necessary to spend. The average price is $550 to $660 including GST. And annually I pay $220 to $330 for pest treatment and prevention. The property inspection at settlement includes pest inspection, structure inspection, water leaking and drain system inspection.

The property inspection is provided by a third-party licensed property inspector. This is different to the banks' valuation. In my property investor club, we seek and recommend good providers without any kick back.

This is like maintaining your own teeth. If you spend $200 to clean your teeth and annual health check, you may have very good teeth. But if you do not do annual teeth check, in the fifth year, or the eighth year, you may have major problems; a root canal treatment for instance may cost you $3,000, and is much more painful.

One of the very sad things is there is lack of transparency in this market. Only in Canberra does the regulation require every vendor to prepare the property inspection report for all potential buyers as part of their sales contract. Whoever buys the property in the end will then reimburse the vendor. But in other states, some agents do not like the fact their potential buyers want to do property inspections, because inconveniences the agents selling the properties. There are many sales falling through because the purchasers found there were serious issues with the properties, but the vendors chose not to fix it. And the $550 inspection fee cannot be refunded. So, whoever is the next buyer without knowing it will be the unlucky one.

A.6. LMI (Lending Mortgage Insurance) – 2%
Usually when buying a house with less than a 20% deposit, you can choose to pay around 2% insurance.

Lenders Mortgage Insurance (LMI) is insurance that a lender takes out to insure itself against the risk of not recovering the outstanding loan balance if you, the borrower, are unable to meet your loan repayments and property is sold for less than the outstanding loan balance.

There are two common mistakes made when considering LMI:

1. What is 'capitalised LMI cost'? How is the LMI paid and charged? Say the LMI is 2%, and you are only required to have a minimum 10% deposit, you are actually still required to pay the 2% at settlement, so you need to prepare a minimum of 12% savings plus all other associated government costs. Many people misunderstand this as meaning that they only need 10% plus all other government costs, and the 2% is included in the loan for future repayment. It is an upfront insurance premium to be paid. You should have it ready on the date of settlement.

2. Do not just focus on saving the interest rate; each bank quotes LMI premiums very differently. You may choose the bank with 0.1% lower rate for a $400,000 loan, which means that you are saving $400 a year. But that bank may charge you $10,000 total LMI cost, compared with the other bank that may only charge you $8,000 LMI, but with 0.1% higher interest rate. So as a rational investor, we need to consider the bigger picture on overall costs, and terms and conditions.

A.7. Insurance Cost – assume $1,000 per property per year
If you will not drive without car insurance, you should not invest a property without landlord insurance, preferably including building insurance. It is just as dangerous.

The price is roughly $800 to $1,200 for a $600,000 investment property, depending on the replaceable value and rental yield. And there are many other factors, such as location, your own profile, claim history, and so on.

Holding Costs For An Investment Property In Australia

Things happen; in my ten-year banking career, I have seen people's houses that were significantly damaged by flood, storm, fire, car accidents, or even job losses which result in an inability to pay the rent. It may be a cost you cannot afford without insurance protection.

Please ensure you read the Product Disclosure Statement or have a good insurance broker explain it to you. You get what you pay for. So, there is no money to be saved. If you choose the cheapest insurance that covers nothing, it is the most expensive in the long run. And my investment club also provides insurance broker services.

It is a tax-deductible cost, so why not spend it wisely?

A.8. Buyers' agents vs. property advisors
There are many busy and rich people out there, usually business owners, doctors, lawyers and those in professional services. They do not have the time to look for an investment property, and they do appreciate other people's professional service as well, seeing the value in opportunity cost. So, they are willing to pay 2% of the property price or $15,000 minimum to pay an experienced buyers' advocate to find the property that they would like to invest in. These people believe, if they bought the wrong investment property, they may lose more than 2%. Or that if they do not take action for a year, the property price may increase by 7.2% for the next year.

I have personally used property buyers' agent before with no regret because that was my busiest time and I wanted to take action. If you want to save that $15,000 buyers' agent fee, then it seems more valuable to do your property search in more detail.

However, a property advisor is different from buyers' agent. Property advisors usually sell off the plan a new property. Buyers' agents usually gets paid by the buyers, and receive no payment from the vendor, otherwise there is a conflict of interest. Property advisors get the commission from the builders or the developers for 2% to 4% of the property price, or $20,000 to $40,000 per property.

Someone is going to pay the bill, but you make the judgement of who is serving your best interests. I am not suggesting that using a property advisor is wrong, because many of them are seeking more premium and suitable properties for investors, rather than just selling random properties for whatever they have. It is a more niche file. Sometimes they will charge a $3,000 to $6,000 membership fee or course fee as well, to educate the investor about how to differentiate between good investment properties.

A.9. Depreciation Report for new property or newly renovated property – assume $550
Typically, you could expect to pay between $385-$770 for a depreciation schedule. The fee you'll pay will vary based on the property type, location, and complexity. $500-600 is a fairly standard price for an established, residential home.

A property depreciation report is a report prepared by a quantity surveyor that saves property investors money. In essence, property investors can claim the wear and tear

Holding Costs For An Investment Property In Australia

of property investment, just like a business can claim the depreciation of the computer they use for their business.

You can claim a lot of tax back for years with one report only.

Again, in my property investment club, you get a bulk price discount through reputable depreciation companies.

A.10. Set up cost of a company or family trust as the holding entity – assume $2,200

Sometimes more sophisticated property investors choose to invest with family trust. Each investor's tax situation and family members are different. It is better to invest in property under family trust for some investors. If they do choose to invest in this way, they need to set up the paperwork in advance.

Accountant cost to set up a family trust on average is $2,000 to $3,000 and an $800 to $1,200 annual tax return fee. This may seem a lot, but it may save them a lot more capital gain tax in the near future.

A.11. Time you need to allocate on searching a property – as a rich habit or as serious as a second job

Buying an investment property and running it is like a second job, or at least you need to treat it as seriously as a second job. Sometimes people feel frustrated or lost because they did not spend the minimum time to master the basic knowledge and process of property investment. You do not just buy one and leave it there for ten years and make profit. You cannot duplicate this system. It is not as simple as that; you need to have a long-term strategy in place.

I would suggest a minimum 20 to 100 hours search to set up the basic knowledge, such as your budget, shortlist locations, setting up the family trust, getting a preapproval, etc, as well as an ongoing four to eight hours weekly to look for a particular property you may like to invest in, one at a time. This may include web browsing on Real Estate.com.au, calling agents, inspecting the properties, and attending the auctions over the weekends.

A.12. Opportunity cost and FOMO
Opportunity cost is the forgone benefit that would have been derived from an option not chosen. To properly evaluate opportunity costs, the costs and benefits of every option available must be considered and weighed against the others.

It simply means if you do not act and invest now, you may miss out on the wave of property price increase. If you also believe in the historical data, we always hear that 'the property price goes up every ten years', and the property price increases by 7.2% on average. So, if you are financially ready, and you really want to get in this game, you need to be mentally ready and equipped with the right knowledge and engage with the right professionals.

Costs of holding an investment property

B.1. Mortgage repayment - plan for the long-term
In Australia, most loan products have a 30-year loan term. Through a statistic in 2015 from Westpac, where I used to work, the average life for a loan is 7.5 years. People may

Holding Costs For An Investment Property In Australia

discharge because they refinanced or sold the property. So, you need to estimate this cost at least for seven years.

This is one of the largest costs, especially at the beginning of holding a property. And the rate is hard to predict. In fact, do not try to predict the interest rates; instead, try to control your own budget at the time of economic cycle.

One of the secrets not many brokers and bankers sit down and discuss with their clients is the assessment rate. They only want to discuss the promotion rates and cash back with the clients so they can get their business today. So, what is assessment rate? Assessment rate is basically a stress test to determine the applicant's ability to repay the loan in the long-term - bear in mind this is a 30-year loan.

I have seen a so-called 'property advisor' presenting a nice excel spreadsheet to one of my friends, saying that a 3% interest-only rate and repayment forever will make that investment property so profitable. But the problem is, it is a fake assumption without referring to the historical data of mortgage rates in Australia and ignoring the terms and conditions that the lender or bank can choose not to renew the interest-only repayment after a certain year. What if the rate is 5.5% and principal plus interest? Then that property advisor is leaving all the pressure on my friend, after they earn the one-off commission. In my career, I have seen property investors letting some properties go in a bad time in the property market; that means they are not selling it at the peak or best price possible, or upper side of the property cycle, simply because their banks no longer can renew their five-year interest-only terms, due to banks' policies or clients' circumstances changing.

Always have a best scenario and worst-case scenario forecast and have a back-up plan for it.

In general, look at the average Australian mortgage rate in the past ten years, which is giving the lenders an indication about whether the borrower can comfortably repay the loan in ten years' time. Say, for example, today I can get 2.49% interest only for two years with bank A, however bank A is using 5.50% in his background. Assuming that ten years later, you can still afford it when they are charging you 5.50% principal and interest instead of 2.49% interest-only, they will give the proposed loan to you today.

Do not be afraid that there is no control over the rates. There is always historical data you can track as a benchmark. And if the mortgage goes up, usually the rental will be pushed up further and faster as well, as the landlord can pass the holding costs, or the rental usually goes up by 2%-3%. At the same time, the salary is supposed to go up by 2%-3% per year; if not, change your boss.

B.2. Council rates and water rates
Council rate is charged by the council to provide services to maintain the community properties, such as rubbish bins for each household, cleaning the road and maintaining the parks. It is usually between $1,000 to $2,000.

Holding Costs For An Investment Property In Australia

Water rate is not charged by water usages. It is the fee you pay to maintain the water pipe and drainage. It is a few hundred dollars a year depending on your location and house value.

Both of these costs can be estimated in your property contract when you are making the purchase.

B.3. Land tax – never decreases

This is different from council rates. Council rates are charged by the council. Land tax is charged by the State Revenue Office. It accumulates the more properties you own, and as the land value goes up. Each state is different, and different ownership, such as having the title under an individual name, family trust, or self-managed superfund, can be different. Each individual can also be different.

Example for a property portfolio in Victoria under individual name:

Reference: https://www.e-business.sro.vic.gov.au/calculators/land-tax

Accumulated land value (Financial Year 2022)	Land Tax
$500,000	$775
$1,000,000	$2,975
$1,500,000	$6,975
$2,000,000	$12,475
$2,500,000	$20,225
$3,000,000	$27,950
$3,500,000	$40,725

Retire On Rent

And here is how the SRO calculated it. https://www.sro.vic.gov.au/land-tax-current-rates

Land tax general rates (from 2022 land tax year)

Total taxable value of land holdings	Land tax payable
< $300,000	Nil
$300,000 to < $600,000	$375 plus 0.2% of amount > $300,000
$600,000 to < $1,000,000	$975 plus 0.5% of amount > $600,000
$1,000,000 to < $1,800,000	$2975 plus 0.8% of amount > $1,000,000
$1,800,000 to < $3,000,000	$9375 plus 1.55% of amount > $1,800,000
$3,000,000 and over	$27,975 plus 2.55% of amount > $3,000,000

Land tax trust surcharge rates (from 2022 land tax year)

Total taxable value of land holdings	Land tax payable
< $25,000	Nil
$25,000 to < $250,000	$82 plus 0.375% of amount > $25,000
$250,000 to < $600,000	$926 plus 0.575% of amount > $250,000
$600,000 to < $1,000,000	$2938 plus 0.875% of amount > $600,000
$1,000,000 to < $1,800,000	$6438 plus 1.175% of amount > $1,000,000
$1,800,000 to < $3,000,000	$15,838 plus 1.0114%* of amount > $1,800,000
$3,000,000 and over	$27,975 plus 2.55%** of amount > $3,000,000

As you can see in the tables, within the same state and certain ownership structure, the land tax rate increases with higher value. I hope this does not discourage you to invest in more properties, but to plan ahead, and plan smarter, such as by investing in multiple states, considering your personal tax situation, considering title ownership, considering commercial real estate and many others. You cannot avoid the tax, and it only increases by time. And the government can change it accordingly.

However, the land value is not equal to the market price. It is usually lower than the market value in the affordable areas only. But in the luxury suburbs, the land value can be higher than the market price, hence why I personally do not recommend investing in luxury suburbs, unless you are a developer.

B.4. Body corporate fee or strata fee
Whenever you buy a property that will share walls and a common area with your neighbour, such as townhouses, units, or apartments, you may pay less land tax for a small portion of land. Try to avoid expensive body corporate fees and strata fees with very high-density buildings. You are paying for a lot of luxury amenities that you may not utilise, such as a swimming pool, or gym in a big apartment. If your tenant is not using those amenities, you are still paying for it. Furthermore, the lift maintenance could be more and more expensive. Did you know that a lift for a high building costs more than a Ferrari? And the maintenance for an old and high apartment building is increasing every year for the many lifts, air conditioning, and more.

You can request an estimation from the agent in writing in an email when you are buying the unit or apartment. Ensure you put these numbers in your Excel sheet and budget appropriately, especially if the purchase is for investment purposes. You will be surprised how much cashflow the strata fee kills for your investment profit.

The owner's corporation fees for apartment buildings in Victoria are on average $2,000 to $4,000 per annum whereas townhouse fees are typically $1,500 per annum. And many high-rise apartments in the CBD actually require more than $10,000 per year, and this cost is still increasing.

B.5. Accountant cost

As mentioned before, the average I pay for this is $550 to $1,100 including GST per investment property I have. But it really largely depends on each property and investors' own tax situation; the more complicated and more sophisticated it is, the more it will cost.

The best thing to do is to get the quotes from your accountant. Or our property investment club can also recommend you someone capable and reliable.

B.6. Rental income and rental management fee

In New South Wales and Victoria, the average price is 5.5% of the total rental. However, in many other states, it may be higher because the rental yield is generally lower than in Sydney and Melbourne. The percentage may go up to 7%-10%. Of course, if the rental yield is high, then the rental commission can go as low as 4%.

If it is a short stay or Airbnb then the charge will be very different - it can be anywhere between 20% to 40%.

Holding Costs For An Investment Property In Australia

Depending on the agency, you may need to pay additional fees to cover things like:

- Letting and lease renewal. The letting fee is usually based on the property's weekly rent, often around one or two weeks' worth of rent but sometimes more. Lease renewal negotiation is sometimes included in this fee but can sometimes also be charged as a separate fee of $25 to $100.
- Administration fee. This typically ranges from $5 to $10 per month.
- Tenancy database checks. Usually, this is $12 per person.
- File preparation and tribunal attendances. Fees range from around $100 to $200 when there are disputes between tenants and landlords.
- End of financial year statement. $25 to $50.
- Lease transfer fee. This charge ranges from $0 to $500.
- Insurance claims (E.g. if you have a landlord's insurance policy and your tenants left without paying the last month's rent). $0-$150.

B.7. Landlord insurance cost
As mentioned before, this is not only the settlement cost, but a recurring cost every year.

B.8. Maintenance cost
This is one of the hidden costs of having an investment property that a lot of agents do not explain to their clients upfront.

Repairs and maintenance are the category that most often upends investors' best-laid plans. According to research by BIS Oxford, the upkeep of a rental house costs an average of $2,661 per year while a rental apartment costs $1,677 per year. But sometimes those figures are a lot higher.

Here are some popular methods to allocate your maintenance budget:

There is no right or wrong way to budget. But as a general rule of thumb, the following formulas may help you forecast your investment property maintenance costs.

1. The 50% rule suggests that total operating expenses may amount up to 50% of the income your rental property generates. For instance, a monthly rent of $1,000 may incur about $500 as maintenance costs.

2. The 1% rule considers the annual property value. It suggests that total operating costs could take up to around 1% of the property value per year. For instance, if the value of your property is $400,000, then your annual maintenance cost may be around $4,000.

3. 5X rule fuses monthly rental income with annual maintenance costs. Multiply the monthly rent by 1.5 to find the annual maintenance expenses. For instance, a monthly rent of $2,000 will present an annual maintenance cost of $3,000.

Holding Costs For An Investment Property In Australia

Part C. Costs of selling a property

Legal and conveyancing
You need to prepare your sales contract first, and the price will be very similar to when you are purchasing your property.

Agent fee: Sales commission
This is between 1.5% to 3.5% on average, depending on the location and average house price. The more expensive the house is, the lower the rate should be. It is wise to ask for at least three agents to provide you with the sales appraisal and quotes on the commission, and other costs.

Agent fee: Marketing fee and auction fee
Many agents do not disclose the other fees clearly enough. There is a fixed range for auction fees. But there is no upper limit, really. With technology today, you can do a lot of fancy video marketing and online social media marketing. But luckily, to sell an investment property, it is much easier.

In 2020, the average marketing campaign in the Melbourne market cost between $6,500 and $8,000.

In Sydney, the marketing cost can range between $4,500 to $10,000, depending on the property and the advertising schedule, according to Michael Minogue from Laing + Simmons in Woollahra.

If you choose to sell at auction, it will cost another $400 to $1,000.

Renovation cost, styling, and furniture cost

Many agents will say this to you: 'If you want to sell your property at the highest price possible, you need to prepare them in the best possible condition so you can attract the best buyer'.

It is hard to quote on the renovation because each house is in different circumstances. But even to do just the carpet replacement and repaint to attract the owner occupiers, who are more willing to pay higher price, you are looking at $10,000 plus.

To hire furniture for the property inspection and make it look appealing, you are going to spend a few grand here as well.

Bank and finance, bridging loan extra interest rate

You are looking at, on average, a $350 discharge fee, and government deregister fee.

If you do get yourself into a bridging loan, do bear in mind that it will have higher interest costs during the bridging period. And there is more time involvement, time pressure to find the right property within time.

I would try my best to avoid a bridging loan.

Capital gains tax (CGT) after selling

There are many forms of holding entity that you can put on the title. These will mean the application of different land tax every year for your holding costs, and also different tax rates when you are selling your investment property. These include:

Holding Costs For An Investment Property In Australia

- Individual names among spouse
- Individual names among family members or friends
- Company
- Trust with corporate trustee
- Trust with individual trustee
- Family trust vs. unit trust
- Self-managed superannuation fund (SMSF)

The top three most common forms are: individual names, family trust with corporate trustee, and SMSF.

Individual names:
- Pro: You can enjoy a lower land tax threshold when you are holding it. You do not have to pay the accountant company or trust set-up fee. You can enjoy negative gearing if applicable.
- Con: You pay the highest individual tax rate when you are selling your property - up to 42% or higher. If you claimed depreciation lost as part of your annual tax return, within certain years if you are selling, you need to give a portion back. When I interviewed a number of multiple property portfolio holders, this was also one of the most common regrets I heard when they were retiring.

Family trust with corporate trustee:
- Pro: You pay 25% tax first when you are selling (note: backer company as beneficiary). And the rest of the after-tax profit, you have the flexibility to distribute to different family members, beneficiaries who got lower individual tax brackets, and furthermore, you also have

the choice to distribute it in different financial years. It can be more complicated and advanced if you wish. Some people have said it is harder to get a loan with a trust and company - I would say they have spoken to the wrong banks or brokers. It sometimes makes the lending easier and more sustainable for long-term growth. In terms of asset protection, many self-employed entrepreneurs and high-risk professionals, such as lawyers, accountants, doctors, prefer to put their assets under non-individual forms or not under their individual names at all to prevent future lawsuits. Just like what Robert Kiyosaki said, 'You do not have to own your assets, but you control them'.

- Con: If you use company as beneficiary, there is no CGT discount. There will be a few thousand dollars set-up cost and ongoing maintenance cost for a good accountant. You cannot claim negative gearing every year, but you can use accumulated costs as the loss against your CGT at the time of selling your property. If the property you invest in has a lot of potential for long-term capital growth, then the accountant fees and negative gearing is most likely worth it.

<u>SMSF:</u>
- Pro: This is probably the only asset class that you do not need to pay any CGT for when you are selling your property. WOW! This is because you are saving the government from having to come up with the budget to be responsible for your retirement. That is a reward for saving hard and investing smart during your work life.

Holding Costs For An Investment Property In Australia

- Con: Terms and conditions apply. There are many restrictions and specifications attached to SMSF. The accountant, auditing cost and mortgage rate are higher. There is also a lack of flexibility, because you cannot refinance and cash out even if the property price goes up. Plus, there is a higher level of entry for equity saving. Usually, it is recommended to have at least $250,000 or more before you set up your own SMSF. You have to hold it until you retire then sell it. Otherwise, you will still need to pay some tax. Also, it is very hard to find the specific property type for SMSF mortgage. It has to be non-construction, high rental yield and with potential capital gain in the long-term.

Of course, you have to consult with your own accountant according to your own personal circumstances to make the right choices for yourself.

I have spoken with so many different accountants, and I would say the knowledgeable ones that are competent enough to provide advice for property portfolio investors are few and far between. So choose them wisely, and consult with respect and curiosity. The good teachers come with good students, who have good questions to ask. It is my dream and goal to set up a professional and unbiased property investment club, with the great professionals we work with. I will also explain in more detail in another chapter about how to work with all different professionals in your property investment journey.

Exercise: Use an Excel sheet to calculate, if you buy a property worth $500,000 today, how much you are going to earn and the costs if you hold it for ten years. Submit it to me via email, and every year we will give out gifts for good Excel spreadsheet readers.

CHAPTER SIX

18 TACTICS TO PAY OFF YOUR LOAN FASTER – SECRETS THE BANKS WON'T WANT YOU TO KNOW- SHORT TERM

Let's start with a fact. Guess how much total interest you will end up paying over a 30-year loan, assuming the loan amount is $500,000 on either a 2.42% rate (average on Dec 2021) or 5% rate (average over the past 10 years), with a $10 monthly fee.

Retire On Rent

Mortgage calculator

How much will my mortgage repayments be?

Mortgage details

Amount borrowed:	Interest rate:	Repayment frequency:
$500,000	2.42%	Monthly

use avg rate (2.42%)

Length of loan:	Fees:	Fees frequency:
30 years	$10	Monthly

Total repayments

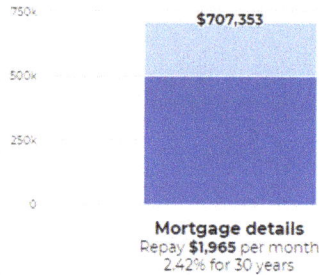

Mortgage details
Repay **$1,965** per month
2.42% for 30 years

18 Tactics To Pay Off Your Loan Faster

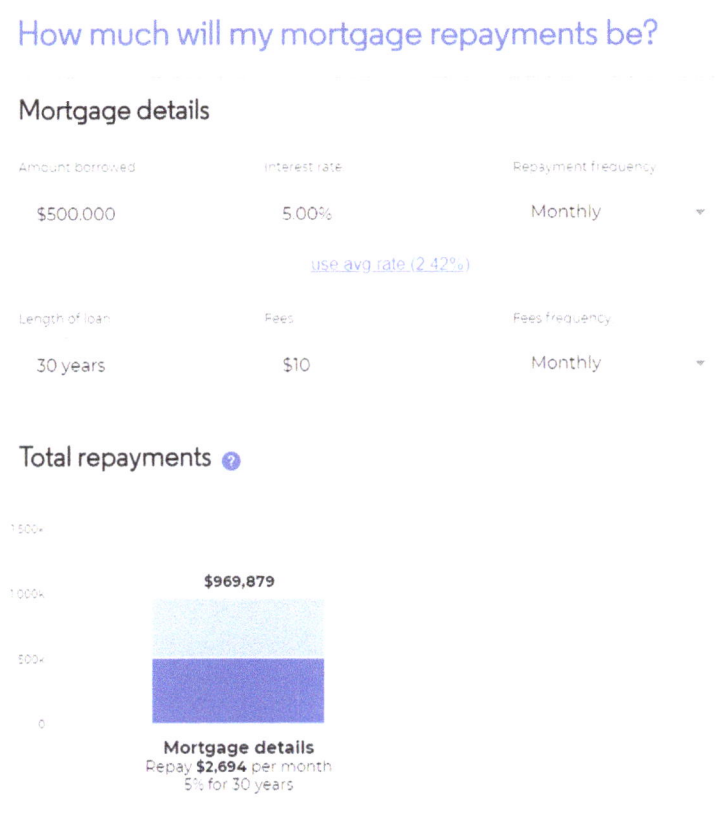

(Source: MoneySmart.gov.au)

You'll pay $207,353 with a 2.42% interest rate, and $469,879 with a 5% interest rate. You are insane if you do not read this chapter!

The banking industry is very busy; it is almost purely transactional driven. Each lending manager in the bank has a KPI (Key Performance Indicator) or target that is related to their bonus. And each broker is paid by each home loan that is settled. All the banks' executives have a three-to-five-year term in their role.

Retire On Rent

The current banking system is designed for immediate gain and short-term results, for its bonus, commission, and share price.

However, you sign up for a 30-year mortgage. On average, the household will keep that mortgage for between seven and ten years. The industry, unfortunately, is not so focused on the long-term, and is weak in financial literacy and financial education for their clients.

Therefore, all property investors need to take the initiative and responsibility to seek ways to look after their own interests. I hate to say this, but it is true that all the investors, consumers, and mum and dad investors, cannot have a victim's mentality. 'I do not know this, I do not know that, someone should tell me this, someone did not tell me that.' Ignorance is not an excuse.

(Cartoon: Banking system, governments, people on a dinner table)

18 Tactics To Pay Off Your Loan Faster

Here is another little secret about how the bank is fattening its profit. They give you a very attractive rate on your loan settlement, then increase your mortgage rate after your loan settles without notifying you. They give the best rate to the new clients and rich clients. The banking system is one of the few industries that treats existing clients worse than new clients. If you have a home loan that has been settled for a couple of years, go to your own banks' official website. You will definitely find a much better rate, but you won't be eligible for it.

The very famous and popular book 'The Barefoot Investor' advises us to call the banks to negotiate the rate after settlement. However, very often these days, the banks' retention team is not willing to make a better offer until they see the discharge form from another bank. A discharge form is a formal document telling your current bank that you obtained a loan offer from another bank, and you can leave now. A lot of times your own banks are testing whether you can really leave or not. Calling your bluff.

In this chapter, I am going to share with you both the tactics and strategies to pay off your mortgage faster. Tactics are the methods to achieve immediate results. Strategies are more a plan to achieve long-term results. I guarantee you, at least at this point, that a lot of this information cannot be found on Google as a comprehensive and systematic theory. You'll only find bits and pieces here and there, or you'll need to pay an expensive fee to listen to someone's seminar. But the seminar will end telling you to borrow up and buy the properties they are selling.

Retire On Rent

Below are the 18 best tactics I would advise using, each of which I have summarised for you:

1. A little extra repayment regularly
2. Once off additional lump sum payment
3. Link your salary and all income source with your offset account
4. Link your credit card with your offset account
5. Separate your main offset account with another daily expense account
6. Invest in a higher return than the offset loan rate
7. Avoid honeymoon rate promotion
8. Increase payment frequency
9. Look beyond big fours
10. Annual financial health check
11. Split your loan into different loan accounts
12. Stay steady with the higher repayment even if the interest rate drops
13. Prioritise your home loan
14. Cut the loan term? Or pay it off quickly?
15. Consolidate your debts!
16. Find out if your profession will give you extra discounts
17. Keep an eye out for hot deals and niche policies
18. Find a good broker

18 Tactics To Pay Off Your Loan Faster

Tactic 1: A little extra repayment regularly

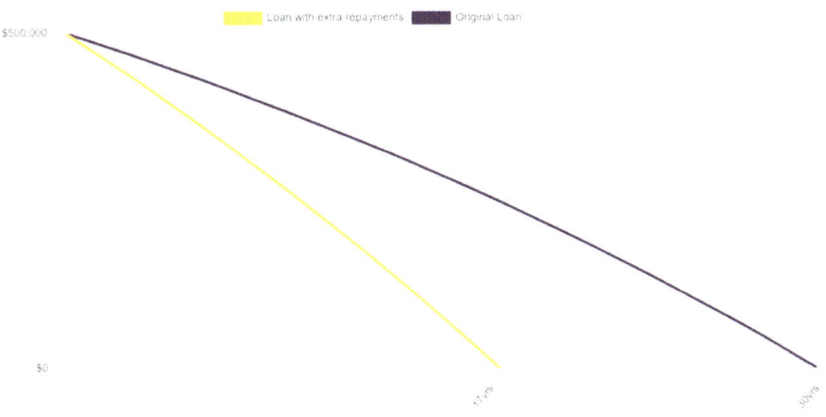

Assumption	Extra Repayment	Years Saved	Interest Saved
$500000 loan	$50 p.m.	1.1 years	$6,393
Rate: 2% p.a. P & I	$200 p.m.	3.9 years	$22,871
30-year loan term	$500 p.m.	9.1 years	$47,233
	$1000 p.m.	22.7 years	$73,302

You can set up automatic extra repayments per month with your direct debit bank. This small extra repayment will drastically reduce the principal and length of your loan term. I will share this Excel tool on my website.

Tactic 2: Once off additional lump sum payment

Lump Sum Payment

My Home Loan

Loan Type
● Variable ○ Fixed ○ Introductory

Loan Amount
$500,000

Loan Period
30 year/s

Interest Rate
5.00 % p.a.

Repayment Frequency
● Monthly ○ Fortnightly ○ Weekly

Your Lump Sum

Lump Sum Amount
$30,000

Lump Sum Payment Made After
5 year/s

Graph | **Yearly Breakdown**

Lump sum principal | Original principal

Year: 6
Lump sum principal: $418,141.69
Original principal: $449,676.55

Monthly Repayments ▶ $2,684.11

Interest you could save ▶ $66,989.99
Time you could save ▶ 3 years 0 months

Assumptions Disclaimer

(Reference: ING Lump Sum Calculator)

What would you do if you received a net saving of $30,000 from your after-tax bonus, a little side business, selling an old car, or a gift from your grandparents? If you choose to make a lump sum reduction of your principal, be mindful this is not to put in the redraw and offset facility that you can take out again immediately - you need to call the bank and adjust the principal.

18 Tactics To Pay Off Your Loan Faster

The above image uses the ING Lump Sum calculator. A $30,000 repayment once-off lump sum, will help you to reduce the loan term by three years, and save you more than double the money you have deposited, i.e. $66,989.99. This is on the assumption that the rate is 5% for a $500,000 limit loan. You can play around with the calculator yourself.

Tactic 3: Link your salary and all income source with your offset account

Firstly, let's introduce how an offset account works. If you have $30,000 extra cash saving, and this is your daily working capital, or emergency fund, that you do not want to use to pay off the loan as a lump sum. You park it in the offset account; your mortgage interest will only be charged the difference between the limit and the offset account balance. But if you do not put the $30,000 saving in your offset account, or redraw facility - say you invest it in shares - then the interest will charge on the total loan amount limit of $300,000.

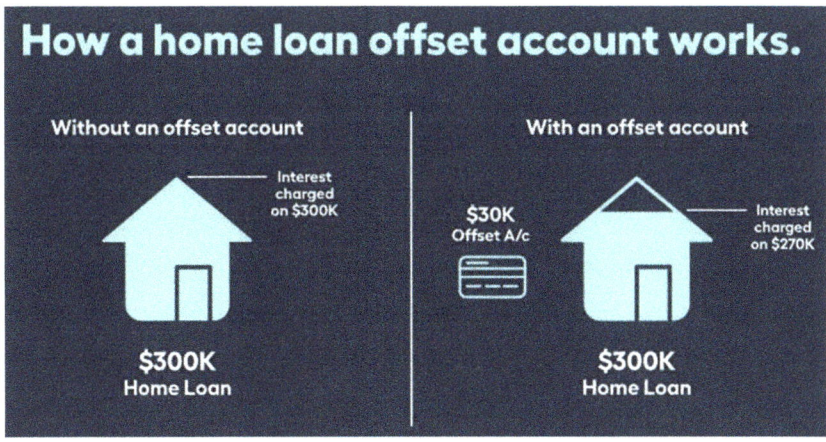

(Picture Source: Great Southern Bank)

Retire On Rent

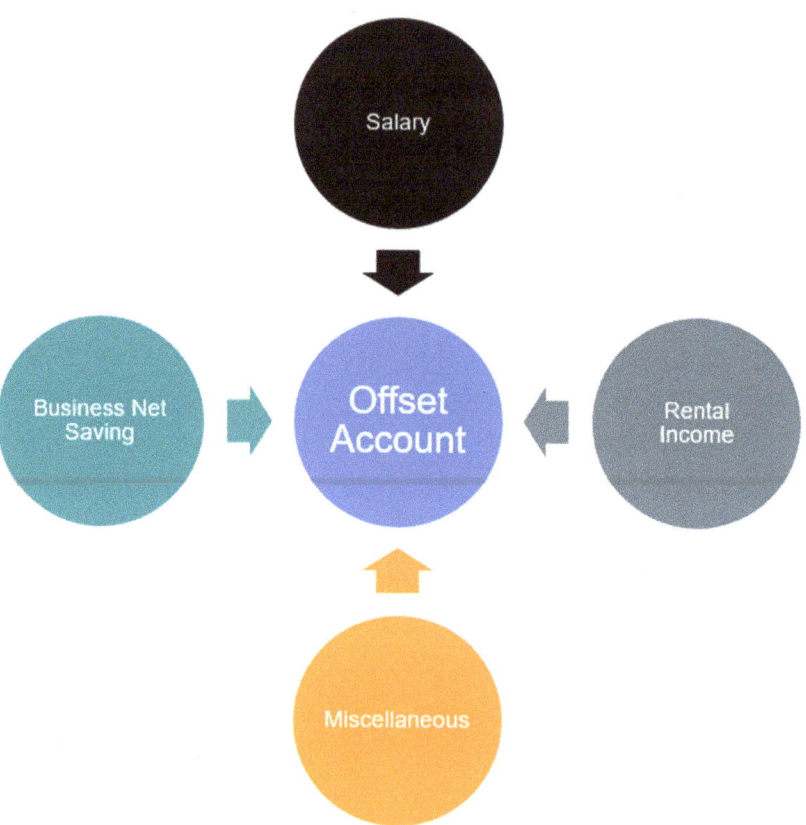

Many people settle their home loan and then forget about it. There are a large number of people who do not utilise the offset account well, or never invest the time to consolidate the accounts linkage and payment direction.

Bear in mind that the interest rate is calculated daily. Here is an example of a couple who each have a gross annual salary of $80,000 a year, so the total joint family income is $160,000 a year. The take home money after tax per month is $10,317.34 (as of FY2020).

18 Tactics To Pay Off Your Loan Faster

Tax withheld for individuals calculator

Tax withheld amount
$1,508

Mr John Citizen

Gross Pay	$6,666.67
Tax withheld	$1,508
Tax applicable	$1,508
Less Tax offsets	$0
Less Medicare levy adjustment	$0
Net Pay	$5,158.67

(Source: ATO tax rate as of 2022 FY, assumptions on no medical levy and no dependants)

If you leave this extra $10,317.34 in your offset account for 30 days, and assuming you are on a 3% interest for a $500,000 loan amount, you are saving $25.79 per month ($309.48 a year). If your rate is 6%, you are saving double at $51.58 per month ($618.96 a year). This saving will automatically make the $395 annual fee or $10 per month ($120 a year) for the offset account worth it. And many banks are discussing waiving the annual package offset account fee now.

Do not underestimate this small amount, because you do not spend all your net salary every month. You will accumulate extra savings. Sometimes you get a pay bonus, overtime, commission, gift money, second job, coins, rental income, salary sacrifice, tax refund, etc. All of this will add up. A small habit will make a powerful compound effect. Here is a little demonstration on how this small habit will save you more than $1,000 a year.

Retire On Rent

Joint Net Income p.m.	$10,317.34	$10,317.34
Loan Limit	$500,000.00	$500,000.00
Interest Rate home loan p.a.	3%	5%
Repayment per month	$2,108.00	$2,684.00
Living Expense	$3,000.00	$3,000.00
Surplus Saving Per Month	$5,209.34	$4,633.34
Accumulate Net Saving Over 2 Years	$125,024.16	$111,200.16

Month	Scenario based on 3% annual interest		Scenario based on 5% annual interest	
	Net Saving	Offset Saving	Net Saving	Offset Saving
1	$10,317.34	$25.79	$10,317.34	$42.99
2	$15,526.68	$38.82	$14,950.68	$62.29
3	$20,736.02	$51.84	$19,584.02	$81.60
4	$25,945.36	$64.86	$24,217.36	$100.91
5	$31,154.70	$77.89	$28,850.70	$120.21
6	$36,364.04	$90.91	$33,484.04	$139.52
7	$41,573.38	$103.93	$36,117.38	$158.82
8	$46,782.72	$116.96	$42,750.72	$178.13
9	$51,992.06	$129.98	$47,384.06	$197.43
10	$57,201.40	$143.00	$52,017.40	$216.74
11	$62,410.74	$156.03	$56,650.74	$236.04
12	$67,620.08	$169.05	$61,284.08	$255.35
Total Extra Saving p.a.		$1,169.06		$1,790.04

How much should I sell my book for if I cannot help you to save your money back? Knowledge is power!!!

Tactic 4: Link your credit card with your offset account

Usually, you will get a free credit card under the package account, which will save you around $300 as a result of not paying the annual credit card fee. Better still, one package can link to multiple properties' loans under the same bank. Some people claim the $395 annual package fee as an investment loan expense as well because it also includes their investment home loans.

18 Tactics To Pay Off Your Loan Faster

The credit card under the package usually comes with the highest reward points and category, such as platinum, black, VIP - sounds very Gucci. The magic feature is a 30 or 45-day interest-free period. So, you can save on monthly living expenses for 30 days and use the credit cards to pay most of your bills, and leave the money to work hard for you in the offset account for that 30-day period. It is not a lot of saving, but it will save back the transaction fee. If the mortgage rate you are offsetting against is 3% or higher, the credit card transaction fee is usually 0.5% to 2%. So, you are saving your money back.

What is more exciting is that those credit card expenses will 'print money' for you in the Reward System. For example, you may have a lot of necessary expenses, such as buying toilet paper, petrol, utilities, and many other regular bills. It is worthwhile looking at the online forums, watching YouTube videos, and reading all these update policies about point systems. The principle is to use the points in exchange for flights and hotels to make the most of it. Even the points system has inflation. If you do not use off the points, their value decreases every year. In terms of the points to real dollar ratio, using it to travel (again on flights and hotels) will have the highest value. If you do not want to travel, you can also take the cash out. Real cash. It is tax-free money.

Some business owners use their business credit cards to cash out points for real cash, while the business expense on the credit cards can still be used as tax-deductible expenses.

I also need to warn you, using a non-physical payment system will encourage overspending because you do not physically see the cash going out from your wallet. So, there are many people opposed to using credit cards and reward cards – instead, they simply use cash to control their spending.

Tactic 5: Separate your main offset account with another daily expense account

18 Tactics To Pay Off Your Loan Faster

This is a psychological game against the smart merchants for those who hate credit cards. Not only can this help you to control spending - for example, by keeping your majority savings and incoming wages in the main account (offset account 1), and deliberately only keeping $1,000 in the minor account (offset account 2). It can also help you to achieve financial information security. Cut the card for offset account 1, set it up for two to sign. Use offset account 2 for your daily expenses, especially online spending. That way, if your card information is stolen, you limit your loss to $1,000.

I will also suggest using offset account 2 for regular expenses and direct debts so you can track what your expenses are monthly. You will be surprised how many unnecessary expenses you may have, such as subscriptions. Unnecessary expense, unnecessary lifestyle. Over the years I have realised, living a less materialistic lifestyle will help me to better achieve freedom both financially and spiritually. You can also use it annually to compare your expenses, such as utilities providers, or determine whether you need change your habits, such as by not eating out too frequently or planting your vegetables in your backyard.

Save the money and spend it on your loved ones.

Tactic 6: Invest in a higher return than the offset loan rate

Fixed rates from
1.84% p.a.
1-year fixed, owner occupied, principal and interest ≤80% LVR

If $50,000 saving
4.35% - 1.84% p.a.
= $1,225 extra taxable income
5.5%
Or 5.5% investment
= $1,830
** not an investment advice

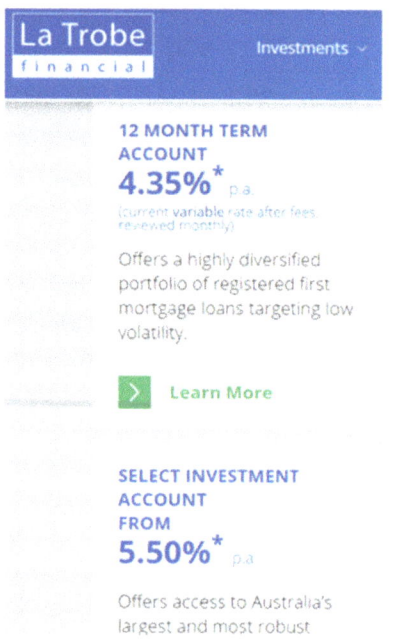

(Source: La Trobe Financial 2021 Investments Products)

In 2021 for example, Mr. John Smith locks in his home loan rate for 1.84% for one year, and he has an extra $50,000 saving for investment. If he selects a mortgage fund at La Trobe Financial for a one-year fixed-term account, assuming 4.35% will not change over one year, then he is earning 4.35% minus 1.84% equal to 2.51% difference on $50,000, which is $1,225 a year. If he selects another investment product at 5.5% return, then he is earning $1,830. You can also use the extra investment income to pay off your mortgage or park it in your offset account.

18 Tactics To Pay Off Your Loan Faster

Of course, this is not investment advice. Everyone has a different risk tolerance and commitment to learn other investments. Do not be too greedy or unprepared.

Tactic 7: Avoid honeymoon rate promotion

(Source: Medium.com)

Some products like this still exist in the market. Be careful with the fine print. It usually comes from some smaller and new-to-the-market lenders, or even big lenders who want to catch up the market share, introducing some base loan products. They promote an incredibly low rate at the first half-year or first few months and increase to a much higher rate afterwards. You may as well get another product, with a relatively lower rate but stable over the long-term. Do not fall into this trap.

Tactic 8: Increase payment frequency

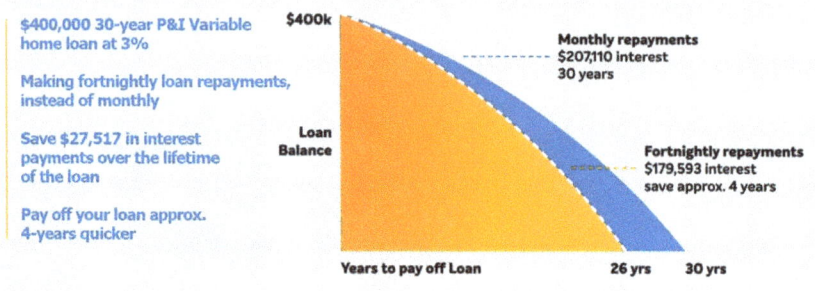

(Source: Bank of Queensland)

Here's a tip that does seem like a magic trick. Most lenders let you make fortnightly (or even weekly) repayments rather than monthly repayments. Because home loan interest is calculated daily, making payments more frequently could help reduce the interest you pay over the term of your loan, helping you become debt-free sooner. By paying fortnightly, you'll end up making one extra repayment per year than if you made repayments monthly.

18 Tactics To Pay Off Your Loan Faster

Tactic 9: Look beyond big fours

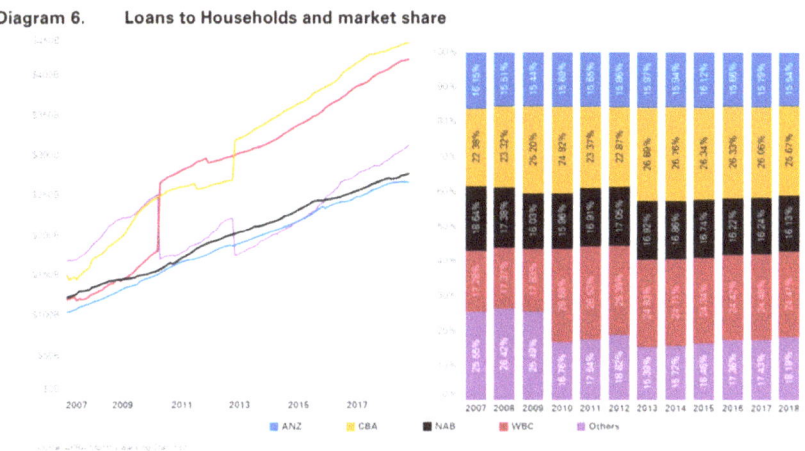

(Source: APRA)

In amazing news, the Macquarie bank settlement on residential loans has become No.2 in the country in 2021. This is the first time an online bank without a branch has overtaken any of the big four.

Get out there and look for a better deal. While many smaller lenders are backed by larger banks, they'll often compete harder for your business. And as well as sometimes offering more personalised services, you may also find that some smaller lenders have home loan options the big guys don't, such as:

- Longer loan terms – for example, 40 years as opposed to 30 years. This will help you to get your first home sooner and start enjoying the capital gains.
- Fixed rate with a 100% offset account.

- Higher loan to value ratios (LVR) without Lenders Mortgage Insurance (usually around $10,000) – this means you may have to pay a lower deposit.
- Reduced application and ongoing fees.
- Lower interest rates.
- May offer home loans to unconventional borrowers (e.g. self-employed or flawed credit).

Tactic 10: Annual financial health check

(Source: www.resourcecenter.cuna.org)

Just like people, home loans need a poke and prod every so often. So never set and forget your home loan. In a tight market, lenders will compete for your business, so take some time every year to do a home loan health check to make sure you're still getting a good deal.

18 Tactics To Pay Off Your Loan Faster

Banks never reward your loyalty, they charge you more interest than new clients, or give you a lower saving rate than new clients.

Negotiate with the retention team, or review your rate with your banker or broker. Threatening to leave may result in you getting extra cash back to stay sometimes.

Of course, if your bank does not treat you as a member or a number, you can always go.

I want to unveil an industry secret here according to my own experience. A lot of bankers have a big staff turnover ratio - 50% of bank staff will not stay in the same position for more than 12 months. They either get promoted, move to different departments or locations, or change to different banks. And 75% of brokers do not continue their business in the second year. The lending manager takes a fixed salary, the mortgage broker takes an upfront commission on loan drawdown and ongoing trial commission for the duration of the loan. The brokers are supposed to have a longer incentive to look after your mortgage. However, sadly, many clients reach out to their brokers after settlement and get no response.

Having a good relationship with responsible brokers will help you to stay below the average rate over the loan term, and of course help you to pay off the mortgage faster.

Tactic 11: Split your loan into different loan accounts

Fix Lower Rate + Variable Rate Combination
(1) for offset variable (2) break down the big goals into small goals;

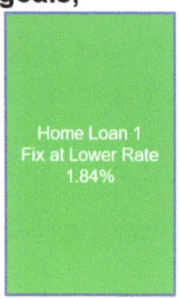

Many borrowers worry about interest rates and whether they will go up but don't want to be tied down by a fixed loan. A good compromise is a split loan, or combination loan as they are often known, which allows you to take part of your loan as fixed and part as variable. Essentially this allows you to hedge your bets as to whether interest rates are going to rise and by how much.

If interest rates rise you will have the security of knowing part of your loan is safely fixed and won't move. However, if interest rates don't go up (or if they rise only slightly or slowly) then you can use the flexibility of the variable portion of your loan and pay that part off more quickly.

The key is not to bet on the mortgage rate going up or down, but to have a flexible structure for all economic weather.

You can also leave a smaller loan account, such as $50,000, as a target to pay off in one or two years. Splitting the big loan into smaller milestones will boost your confidence financially. Once you pay off the $50,000, you can split another $50,000.

18 Tactics To Pay Off Your Loan Faster

So, what's the right loan amount to split as a variable rate with an offset account and option to pay off early? My personal suggestion would be, like in the graph above, to simply use your current savings plus projected savings in the near future.

Tactic 12: Stay steady with the higher repayment even if the interest rate drops
If interest rates drop, don't automatically drop to making minimum monthly payments. It's still a good idea to try to keep repaying your home loan at a higher rate. The extra money will come off your principal which means you are paying off your mortgage sooner.

Make repayments at a higher rate. A good way to get ahead of your mortgage commitments is to pay it off as if you have a higher rate of interest. Get a loan at the lowest interest rate you can and add 2 or 3 points to your repayment amount. So, if you have a loan at about 4% and pay it off at 5%, you won't even notice if rates go up. Best of all, you'll be paying off your loan quicker and saving yourself a packet.

Tactic 13: Prioritise your home loan
When I was working at the bank, sadly I had to call some clients to remind them to make their late mortgage repayment, while they were earning high income but on holiday in Hawaii. This is a good example of not prioritising your home loan repayment.

Freeing yourself from the mortgage monster means keeping your eyes on the prize. Tightening your belt on some of your less important expenses can add up to significant savings over time. For example, do you really need cigarettes or a luxury car?

And make sure all your household services are working hard for you by comparing your electricity and gas, internet providers, or even looking into your health insurance.

There's no point paying for things you don't need, or overpaying for things you do, so find where you can make some cuts. You could use the extra cash to make additional payments on your home loan and help to secure a debt-free lifestyle sooner. I was actually surprised during my career that many really wealthy clients, who were successful in their career or business, were living very humbly, driving an economical car worth less than $50,000 market value and wearing a Casio watch.

What do Australians really spend their money on? Let's compare the national statistics vs. your own budget record and estimation. Think of how good spending habits will help you to get rich. Every bit counts.

18 Tactics To Pay Off Your Loan Faster

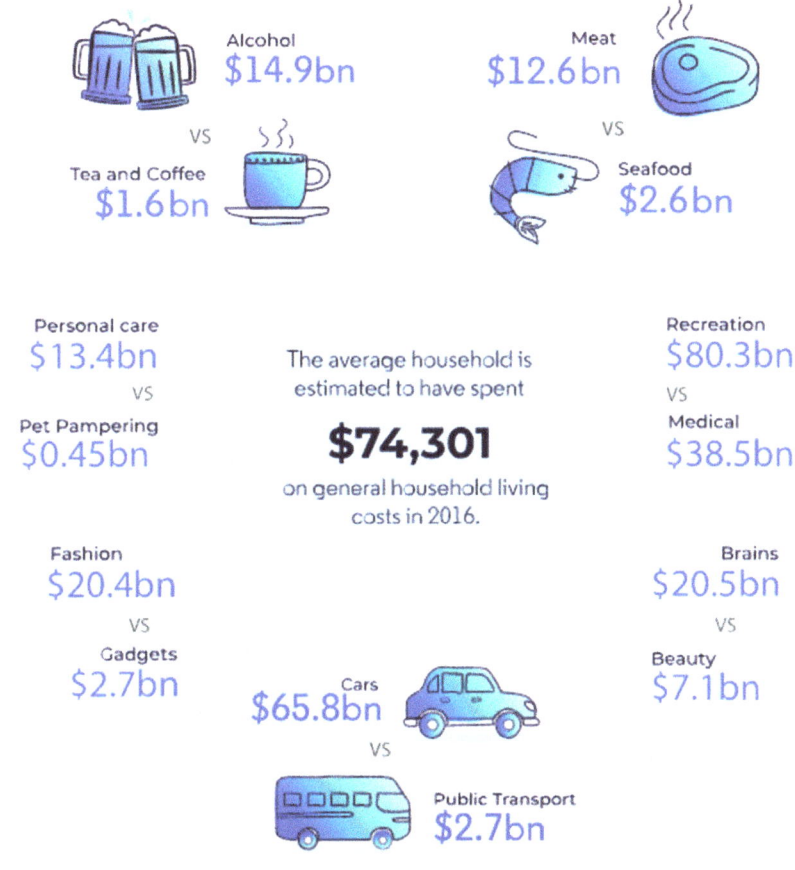

If it was you, how much weight and percentage would you allocate to different categories? What you spend actually represents your values in life. If you invest more money on your brains (i.e. ongoing education and personal development) rather than on your brands and looks, it will actually make you wealthier. Likewise if you concentrate the extra savings on paying off the mortgage than unnecessary 'things'. It would be great, of course, to have everything and have it both ways. However, in most cases, we only have a limited budget, so we need to prioritise, stick to our goals and be disciplined.

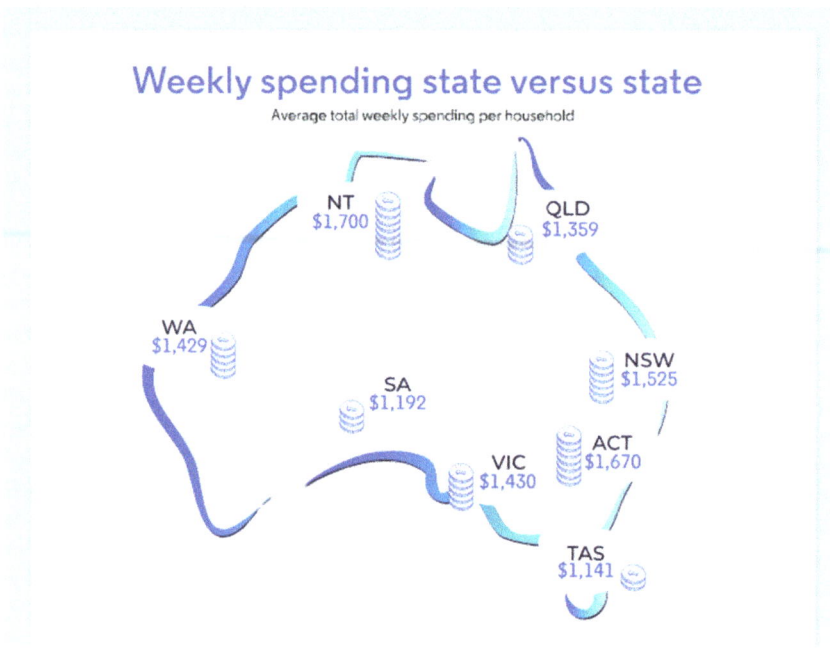

18 Tactics To Pay Off Your Loan Faster

State by state spending on individual items

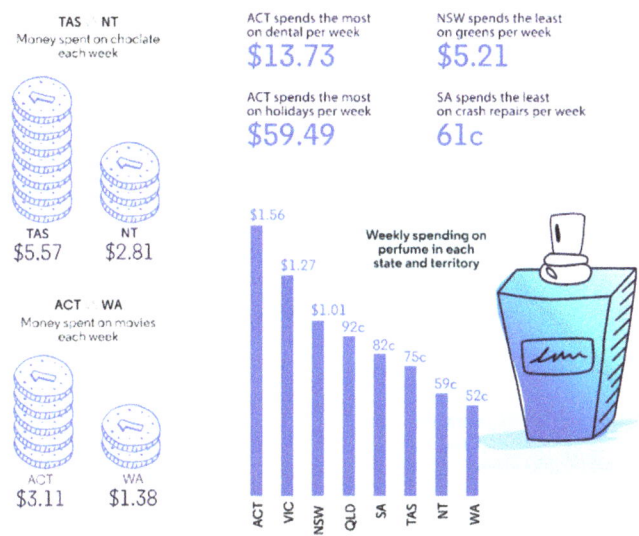

Average weekly Australian household costs

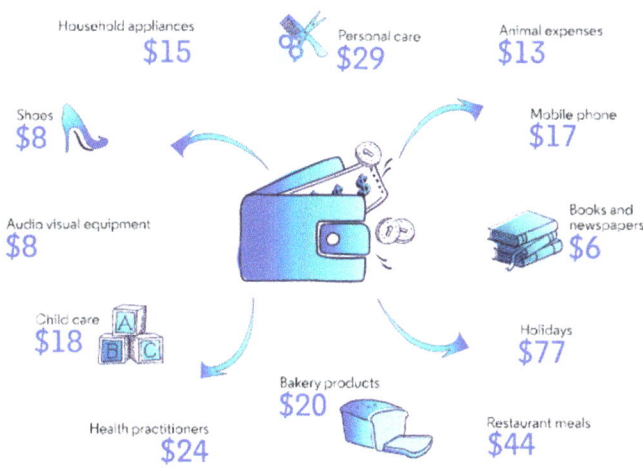

149

Retire On Rent

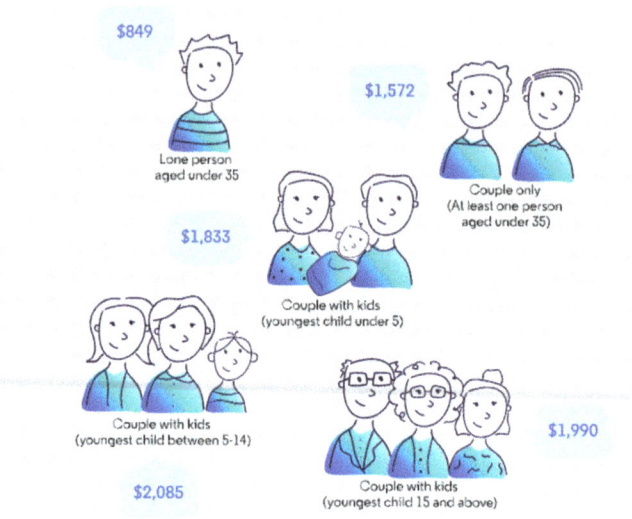

Weekly spend by life stage

	Lone person aged under 35	Couple only (At least one person aged under 35)	Couple with kids (youngest child under 5)	Couple with kids (youngest child between 5-14)	Couple with kids (youngest child 15 and above)
Housing	$284	$381	$458	$355	$359
Fuel and power	$24	$35	$48	$54	$53
Food and drink	$122	$239	$282	$336	$332
Clothing and footwear	$18	$54	$62	$64	$61
Medical and health expenses	$23	$69	$85	$104	$110
Alcohol	$22	$39	$28	$35	$47
Transport	$97	$243	$247	$309	$292
Recreation	$83	$176	$158	$263	$243
TOTAL	$849	$1,572	$1,833	$2,085	$1,990

(Source: smartmoney.gov.au & Source: Australian Bureau of Statistics Household Expenditure Survey, 2015-16.)

18 Tactics To Pay Off Your Loan Faster

Tactic 14: Cut the loan term? Or pay it off quickly?

Loan Amortization Schedule

Enter values		Loan summary	
Loan amount	$ 500,000.00	Scheduled payment	$ 2,108.02
Annual interest rate	3.00 %	Scheduled number of payments	360
Loan period in years	30	Actual number of payments	360
Number of payments per year	12	Total early payments	$ -
Start date of loan	1/1/2018	Total interest	$ 258,887.26
Optional extra payments	$ -		

Loan Amortization Schedule

Enter values		Loan summary	
Loan amount	$ 500,000.00	Scheduled payment	$ 2,772.99
Annual interest rate	3.00 %	Scheduled number of payments	240
Loan period in years	20	Actual number of payments	240
Number of payments per year	12	Total early payments	$ -
Start date of loan	1/1/2018	Total interest	$ 165,517.13
Optional extra payments	$ -		

Time is money. There are all sorts of strategies for paying less interest on your loan, but most of them boil down to one thing: Pay your loan off as fast as you can. For example, if you take out a loan of $500,000 at 3% for 30 years, your repayment will be about $2,108. This equates to a total interest of $258,887 over the term of your loan.

If you pay the loan out over 20 years rather than 30, your monthly payment will be $2,772 a month. But the total interest amount you will repay over the term of the loan will be only $165,517 - saving you approximately $93,370! That's one year's salary for many people. You are saving yourself one extra year of debt free living -- <Retire with Rent>!!

Tactic 15: Consolidate your debts!

One of the best ways of ensuring you continue to pay off your loan quickly is to protect yourself against interest rate rises. If your home loan rate starts to rise, you can be absolutely positive about one thing - your personal loan rate will rise and so will your credit card rate and any hire purchase rate you may happen to have.

This is not a good thing as the interest rates on your credit cards and personal loans are much higher than the interest rate on your home loan. Many lenders will allow you to consolidate - refinance - all of your debt under the umbrella of your home loan. This means that instead of paying 15% to

18 Tactics To Pay Off Your Loan Faster

20% on your credit card or personal loan, you can transfer these debts to your home loan and pay it off at 5% (or whatever rate your home loan is).

As always, any extra repayments or lump sums will benefit you in the long run.

Tactic 16: Find out if your profession will give you extra discounts

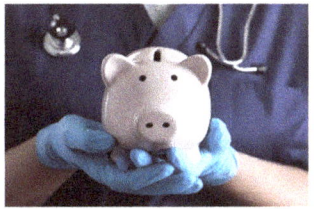

Banks are trying to fight for market share with different ways of marketing. Some job categories will have privileges from big fours or smaller lenders such as community banks for teachers or nurses, etc. Some of the jobs that can enjoy extra discounts and benefits are:

- Doctors
- Dentists
- GPs
- Pharmacists

- Nurses
- Lawyers
- Accountants
- CFA analysts
- Teachers
- Fire Fighters
- Police
- Defence Members
- First home buyers (by category, not by job)

So, while you are working in that job, why not consider taking advantage of it?

Tactic 17: Keep an eye out for hot deals and niche policies
Rates sometimes decrease as well as increase, so keep an eye out for any great rates on offer with one major caveat – check what it will cost you to switch loans. If you do switch to a lower payment, keep up the rate of your old payments to pay the mortgage down more quickly – you'll pay less interest overall and be mortgage-free sooner.

Some promotion and niche examples:

- $4,000 refinance cash back, $2,000 new purchase cash back
- Waive 30 years annual fee ($395 x 30 years = $11,850)
- Fixed rate with 100% offset facility
- Owner-occupied rates for all your investment properties (save 0.2%-0.3% forever)

18 Tactics To Pay Off Your Loan Faster

<u>Tactic 18: Find a good broker</u>

Yes, some of you may be thinking this is too much information already, and you do not have enough time to keep updated with the market on different offers from different lenders. Then, of course, find the right person to save you from hundreds of mistakes and time. Save time and use a professional.

There are not enough good brokers out there. We will have a separate chapter on how to identify a good broker, and also how to identify all different professionals you need in your property investment journey.

Even if I am not a broker one day, I will choose a good one to work for me.

CHAPTER SEVEN

STRATEGIES TO PAY OFF YOUR MORTGAGE FASTER

For me, strategy is something you need a long-term period to achieve. It is not something you can implement now and expect to see the effect within 12 months. In contrast, tactics is something you can apply and see immediate results within 12 months, such as refinancing to lower rates, or adding frequency of repayment.

In the previous chapter, I introduced the most practical tactics to pay your loan off faster. In this chapter, I will outline some of the strategies I personally found helpful. Again, this is not a financial advice piece. I do not know your circumstances, and my advice may not be suitable for everyone. It is based on the personal experiences of mine and many of my successful clients. The market conditions, banks and ATO policies may change from time to time.

For your consideration, some of the most practical strategies from my personal experience and observation from thousands of live cases, are as below:

1. Use a portfolio loan starting from 0.75% interest rate
2. Sell owner-occupied home and downsize with high yield rental properties
3. Buy and hold more now
4. Hold and develop
5. Consider SMSF property investment
6. Consider commercial properties
7. Understand the valuation report and follow the capital gain

1. Use a portfolio loan starting from 0.75% interest rate

Is this possible? Did you make a typo? Are you sure it is 0.75% and not 2.75%? What's the catch?

I am sure I am right. Knowledge is power.

As of March 2022, the average bank's rate is 2.44% according to SmartMoney.gov.au. There are many non-banks or non-big fours trying to provide different and unique products to fight for market share.

Strategies To Pay Off Your Mortgage Faster

You can get 0.75% for your owner-occupied home if you fit the the following criteria:

1. You have more than one property.
2. Your investment loan amount is more than your owner-occupied home loan amount.
3. You are willing to pay higher interest on an investment loan up to 4.95% in exchange for a 0.75% owner-occupied rate.
4. You are a big fan of 'Good debt' vs. 'Bad debt', which means you prefer to pay off your own home faster because it is not tax-deductible.
5. You earn high taxable income and exchanging higher investment property mortgage rates will help you off more tax.

There is more than one lender offering this kind of product now, Mortgage Mart being just one example.

Retire On Rent

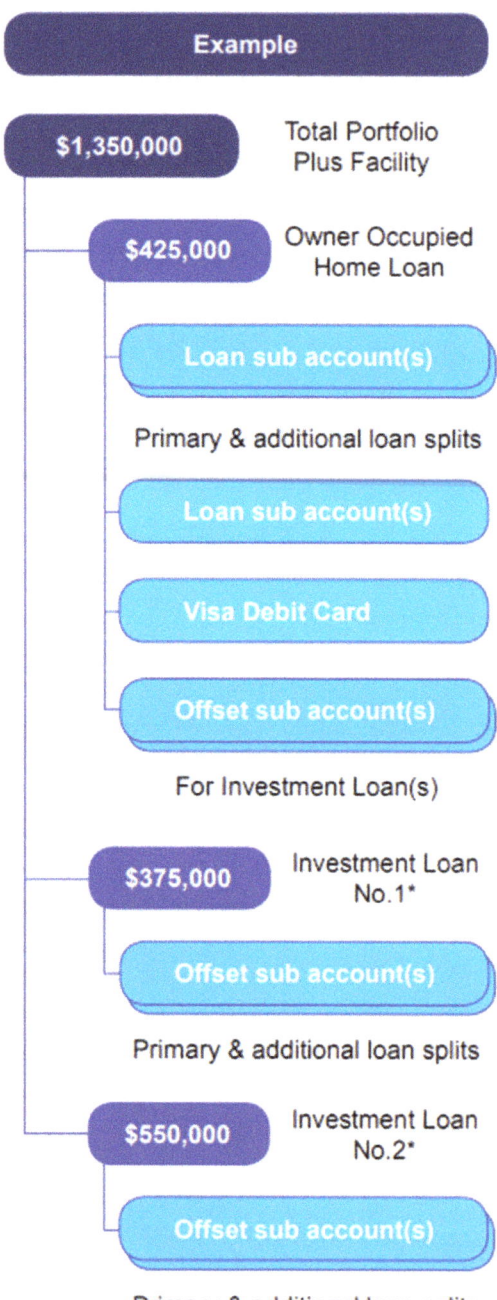

(Reference: www.mortgage-mart.com.au/portfolio-plus/)

Strategies To Pay Off Your Mortgage Faster

Taking The Portfolio Plus Loan Facility from the lender Mortgage Mart as an example, its standard variable interest rate is 2.99%. In the example above, the effective variable interest rate applicable to the owner-occupied home loan, after the customer loyalty rebate, would be 0.75% with a saving of approximately $11,050 in the first year. This is for illustrative purposes only.

I will show you another secret that the banks never want you to know. An amortisation table refers to the repayment of principal and interest breakdown to gradually pay off the home loan. However, in Australia, there is only one way to pay the principal off, which is called 'interest forward loading'. This simply means you are paying most of the interest at the earlier year of the mortgage. That is the secret to how the banks earn a lot of money from you.

You have to remember this concept.

If you have a $425,000 owner-occupied home and a $1,350,000 investment loan, in any of the big fours, the interest rate you can get as of today is around 2.19% for the owner-occupied home (base loan without offset account) and 2.79% for the investment loan with base loan without offset account. Or, if we compare apples to apples, for example a package loan with an offset account in any big four, the average rate today is 2.49% for owner-occupied, or 3.09% for investment loan. All of this is with principal and interest repayment and variable rate.

Let's take the example of using the portfolio loan product and paying 0.75% on your owner-occupied home. Here is the amortisation table breakdown for the first 12 months. In the red box, you can see the total interest is only $49,736.20. And in the blue box, you can see the portion of principal and interest each month. Mostly it is principal.

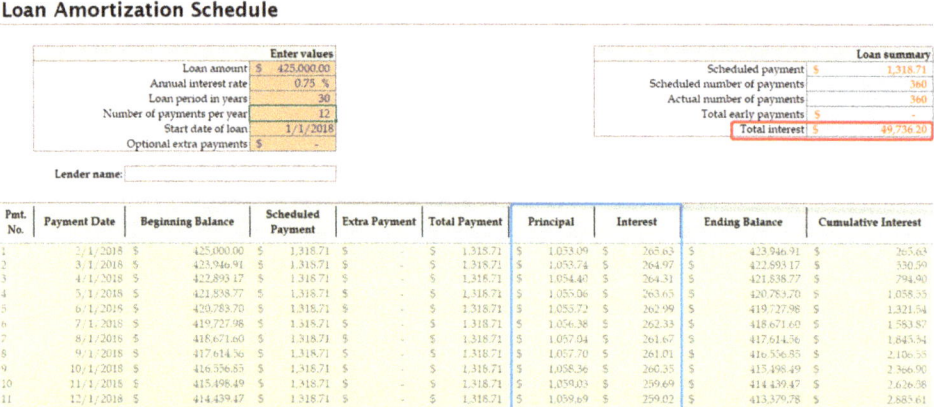

Now, taking the example of most clients, who choose the normal banking products, and take no human advice, they are paying $178,739.80 over the loan term, which is more than three times the previous product (approx. 3.6 times more). And in the blue box again, you can see how the interest rate will affect the principal and interest portion. This is the bad debt that does not help with offsetting your high tax ratio.

Strategies To Pay Off Your Mortgage Faster

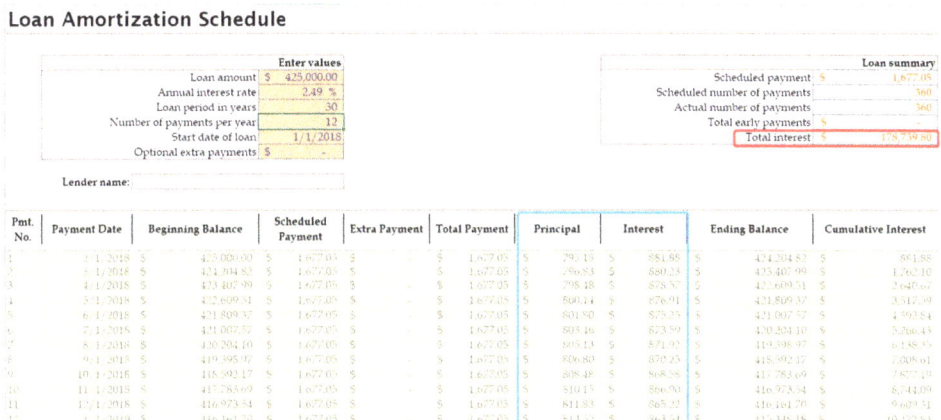

Let's look at both sides of the portfolio. For an investment loan, if you are using 4.95% higher investment rate vs. 3.09% normal investment loan rate, it seems like you will be paying a lot more interest, which is approx. $521,000 over 30 years. And if you compare the repayment each month, it is approx. $2,000 extra.

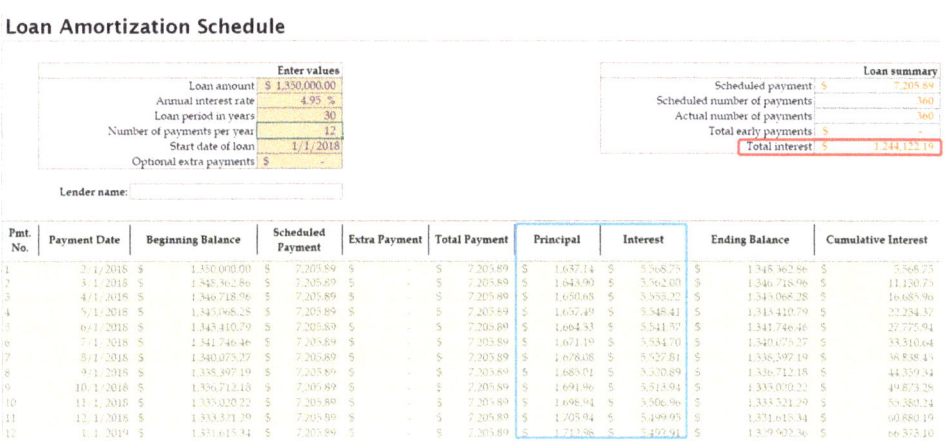

Retire On Rent

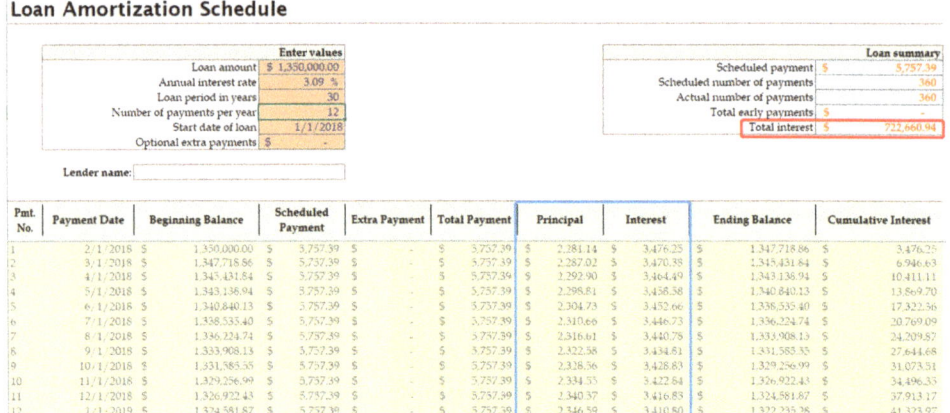

Now, some of you may get confused. It is OK to take this to your accountant, remembering that each person has a different tax situation. If this is helping you to build up more negative gearing or accumulated loss as tax benefits, it may suit you as it claims back a lot of tax for you. So, paying more investment interest here does not necessarily mean it is bad, because the investment mortgage rate is 'good debt'.

For some, it's more beneficial to use portfolio loans, as they pay less on owner-occupied home loans, claiming more tax back. It is about thinking outside the box. The product exists and is increasing in popularity for a reason.

After you smash off your owner-occupied property, you can still refinance the portfolio back to a normal bank lower investment loan rate. Furthermore, you then can cash out from your owner-occupied home again for investment purposes, and its interest cost will be tax deductible again.

The benefits build up.

Strategies To Pay Off Your Mortgage Faster

A disclaimer worth mentioning again and again - financial and interest rate and policies are as of today. It may change over time.

2. Sell owner-occupied home and downsize with high net yield properties

Yes, you are right, the sentence itself is very self-explanatory. Many people will only buy one property for their whole life, and they can still achieve the 'retire with rent' goal.

Some people do not live for money, never aiming to be materially wealthy. Included among this group would be people in professions such as nurses and teachers, who I always think are underpaid.

Firstly, you do not pay any capital gains tax when you sell your owner-occupied home. So, for example, if you purchase a house that is worth $600,000, and you work for 30 years as a teacher, and the house price doubles every 10 years, then 30 years later, you pay off your mortgage, and the house is worth $4.8 million today. Selling off your $4.8 million property will allow you to buy a lot today. You can buy a decent-sized apartment with $1 million, and with the rest of the $3.8 million cash, even without getting a loan, you can still invest in small apartments or studios, with less land tax and less corporate maintenance fee. Let's say you are buying five medium-sized apartment, producing $20,000 net rent each property, that is $100,000 rental income per year. Or you can also buy another house with lower rental yield but higher capital growth opportunity.

Retire On Rent

Secondly, I hope you pay attention to the key word - house. You bought a house 30 years ago, that is an achievement. Not an apartment, or townhouse. Look up realestate.com.au for any recent sales, then search their purchased price 30 years ago. You will be amazed by the power of compounding. However, many young home buyers do not see the value in the land component, and rush into apartments and townhouses for their first home. These are more suitable for short-term living, and you're better off renting them out and buying another house to hold. Most people do not think that their owner-occupied home is actually one of their best investment vehicles in Australia, because there is capital gains tax.

Thirdly, maintain financial discipline for 30 years. This is hard. This strategy sounds so simple, but most people cannot achieve it. Australia has a 50% divorce rate, and many people divorce more than once. I found some people will not sell their home during the separation. One of the parties will refinance and change the ownership from two to one person on the title, even if it's with cash to pay the other party out. This at least keeps the property for one of the parties and helps to avoid paying stamp duty again when buying new property. Also, the property price will already have increased a few years after the separation, so they could never afford the same size house in the same suburb for the same price. People have freedom of choice with regards to divorce, but I just hope people do it more rationally with more financial consideration. Apart from divorce, there is also overspending, such as Afterpay, Zip Pay, credit card, etc. I could never appreciate the concept; despite how well-performing its share price is. I simply believe it is a product that takes our generation backwards. Do not spend the money you do not have.

Strategies To Pay Off Your Mortgage Faster

3. Buy and hold more

It is very funny that some seminars say, 'Come in and we will teach you how to pay off your loan faster,' but you walk out with one more property, which is eventually more debt, after all.

Well, I guess there is nothing wrong with that, if all your property prices increase after time, and your mortgage decreases after that. As long as the cashflow is manageable through time.

It is very similar to strategy No.2; investors choose this strategy and are usually more comfortable dealing with mortgage and leveraging throughout their investment journey. There are definitely benefits to this, and their property portfolio will most likely grow faster.

For example, if the previous owner bought the $600,000 property 30 years ago, and every ten years his income increased, then by using the increased income to cash out and purchase another investment property, and repeating this every ten years, an investment portfolio of eight properties is possible.

Retire On Rent

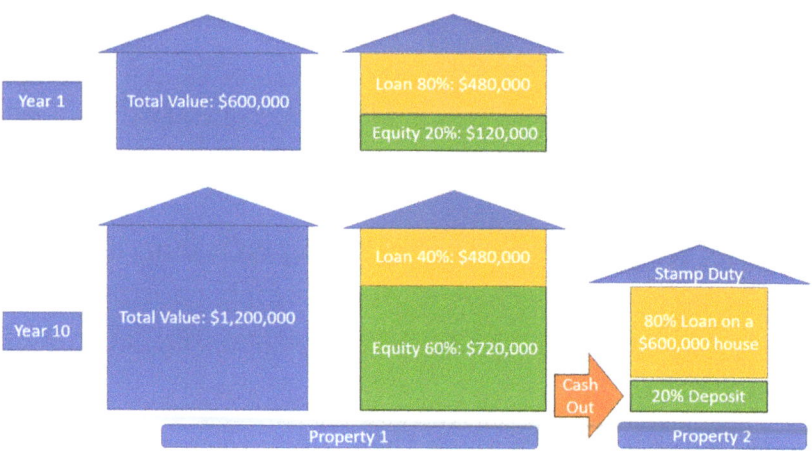

Even if he uses interest-only all the time, and keeps the loan amount the same for ten years, ten years later the property price has doubled and he can cash out from the first property and buy the second one. The assumption of course is the property and asset value always go up, and his income also goes up a lot by time. By the time he sells his owner-occupied home without capital tax again, he will definitely have a few more investment properties without the debt.

Strategies To Pay Off Your Mortgage Faster

4. Hold and develop

To get eight investment rental incomes, you do not have to wait for 30 years to buy eight properties - you can simply buy two and develop four on each. This will take you less than 30 years, hence the word 'development' and it is an escalating strategy for rent book accumulation.

There are many build and hold strategies:
1. Knock down and build up to four townhouses or units on a piece of land (up to four otherwise it cannot be recognised as a residential loan product, but rather a commercial loan facility).

2. Do not knock down the old building, but do a land subdivision on the large block, for an extra house or two smaller units at the back and renovate the old house at the front.

This strategy is about adding value to the existing land. You can wait until the house price goes up, and cash out from the existing increased equity, and apply 100% funding for the construction. You are getting a new property without paying extra stamp duty.

However, knowing good builders and understanding land subdivision, planning and permit, is another very big topic to learn.

5. Consider SMSF property investment

There are only two kinds of property that can be exempt from paying capital gains tax. One is our own home; the other is a property under the self-managed super fund. Again, this is not suitable for everyone, as different families have different family members and relationships, sizes, risk appetites, incomes and equity positions, retirement plans, etc. So, it is best to speak to your financial planner to see if this strategy will suit you.

The government's intention is to encourage people to look after themselves for their own retirement rather than relying on the government for pension, so the government gives this tax benefit.

A lot of people start considering investing in property under SMSF 10 to 15 years before their planned retirement age. Some investors prefer property over shares, because it provides less fluctuation - it is in bricks and mortar, something they can touch and see. This is especially true for those who have lost a lot of

Strategies To Pay Off Your Mortgage Faster

money in the share market before, or those who went through the GFC, the depression, and witnessed some public listed companies just going bust. Property is not perfect, it is less liquid, but the money in SMSF is there for the long-term anyway. People will not intend to sell it until they retire. Holding it for 10 to 15 years or longer is more than enough to see its value double or triple for a lot of chosen suburbs and chosen properties.

Imagine you purchased a property under your SMSF for $700,000 today, and you borrow 60% (for SMSF the interest rate is higher than normal residential rate, and lower gearing limit). The rental is just enough to cover the interest repayment. If we assume that property in that suburb would double every ten years, it is then on average 7.2% per year growth. You hold it from 45 to 60 years old. So, with 7.2% growth per year for 15 years, the value will be approx. $1.986 million. If we excluded all the other minor holding costs, you would enjoy another $1.286 million net profit without capital gains tax.

Let's look into it from another perspective. To purchase this property worth $700,000 today, you need to contribute a 40% deposit plus let's assume the highest stamp duty in Australia, which is Victoria at 5.5%, and there is a $10,000 set up cost for the family trust and finance. $700,000 x 45.5% + $10,000 = $328,500.

$1,286,000 profit vs. $328,500 cash investment on day one - this is 3.9 times growth. Many people in the finance analysis industry will use different concepts to analyse this, such as cash-on-cash return, or IRR or ROI. You can do your own fancy maths; I invest with common sense.

How can this help you to pay off your mortgage faster? This is low-hanging fruit, a very profitable option and accessible for most people. SMSF property investment helps you to earn more profit to pay off your loan, unlike those profits from selling normal investment properties which have to bear a lot of tax, decreasing your return.

Of course, understanding the risk in tax regulation change, SMSF policy changes, property market, property selection, lending policies change and economic outlook, is also important.

6. Consider positive cashflow commercial properties

Many investors will face the same challenges during their property investment journey. They have enough equity and savings, but they do not have enough income to service more loans, so they cannot continue investing in the property market.

That is not true in the commercial property space. Welcome to the new world.

This is one of the most popular investment options for many Jewish families with history around the world. Here are a few advantages of investing in commercial properties:

1. Purchasing a commercial property with a third-party long lease will not require your personal income for servicing, as long as you have enough deposit.

2. It is usually a positive cash flow investment. The bank loan requires it to be positively geared. For example, if the bank requires a 1:2 interest cover ratio, it means every $1 interest-only repayment will require $2 net rent to service. So at least you will get positive rent to pay the land tax, income tax, insurance, interest, etc. In most cases, it is still positive cash flow after all fees are deducted. So, it is easier to use the rental income to pay off the mortgage by itself after time.

3. A commercial lease is usually much longer than a residential lease. It is usually five to fifteen years or longer. It provides more stability in long-term rental income.

4. There is nil inheritance tax in Australia if you want to pass it on to your children.

In a nutshell, due to lower gearing at the beginning and long-term tenancy, the positive cashflow can pay off the debts by itself.

7. Understand the valuation report and follow the capital gain

For most people, we do not have the time to go through another university degree for a two-year Master's Degree in Property Analysis, or a three-year Bachelor for Property Investment course. However, we can learn the thinking framework in just a few minutes.

The secrets all lie in your property valuation report. Usually, the bank will not share a copy with you - they are trying to keep it for themselves for mortgage purposes and avoid the argument with you.

However, most independent valuers are open to the public nowadays. They charge a very affordable rate, from a few hundred dollars for residential properties, to a couple of thousand dollars for commercials. You can pay them for the report for non-mortgage purposes, just market analysis or buyer advice, or tax purposes. The beauty of it is that the thinking framework is very logical and comprehensive. An expert with a university degree with many years of industry experience will explain to you about property market price comparison, market risk, legal risk and so on. You can refer to a table of contents below, from one of the valuation reports.

Strategies To Pay Off Your Mortgage Faster

TABLE OF CONTENTS

1	Executive Summary	4
1.1	Valuation Assumptions	7
1.1.1	Critical Assumptions	7
1.1.2	Verifiable Assumptions	7
2	Risk Analysis	9
2.1	Property Risk Rating	9
2.2	SWOT Analysis	9
2.3	Investment Analysis	10
3	Introduction	11
3.1	Instructions	11
3.2	Definitions	11
3.3	Date of Valuation	11
3.4	Independence of Valuer	12
3.5	Information Sources	12
4	Property Details	13
4.1	Legal Description	13
4.2	Town Planning	13
4.3	Location	14
4.4	Site Details	14
4.5	Statutory Assessment	15
4.6	Utilities	16
4.7	Environmental, Heritage and Cultural	16
5	Improvements	17
5.1	Description of Improvements	17
5.2	Services	17
5.3	Accommodation & Internal Finishes	18
5.4	Onsite Parking	18
5.5	Building Areas	19
5.6	Building Condition and Utility	19
5.7	Occupational Health & Safety/Essential Services	19
6	Tenancy Details	20

7	Financial Analysis	21
7.1	Income Summary	21
7.2	Outgoing Expenses	21
8	Market Commentary	21
9	Market Evidence	23
9.1	Rental Evidence	23
9.1.1	Rental Summary	24
9.2	Sales Evidence	24
9.2.1	Sales Summary	29
10	Valuation Methodology	30
10.1	Highest and Best Use	31
10.2	Capitalisation Approach	31
10.3	Direct Comparison	33
10.4	Summary of Valuation Approaches	34
10.5	Sales History	34
10.6	Selling Period & Marketability	34
10.7	Suitability for Mortgage Purposes	34
10.8	Insurance Estimate	35
10.9	Valuation Qualifications	35
11	Valuation	37

- Appendix 1: Letter of Instruction

- Appendix 2: Certificate of Title and Plan

- Appendix 3: Planning Property Report

(**Reference**: One of the valuation reports on a property provided by an independent valuer. The content cannot be disclosed due to privacy consent. However, you can all purchase one for your own properties for learning purposes.)

Once my mentor taught me that it is not you buying the property, but rather the bank that is buying the property. You only paid 20% for most cases - the banks pay the majority. And the banks rarely lose the money. Valuation report and system is one of the most important risk mitigation tools for them to prevent market risk.

Also, more importantly, you need to learn how the banks look at the economic and property market. Which suburbs, industry, tenants and property types do the banks favour? Seek the clues for capital gain, because that's where your future profit is, and that's the future opportunity for you to refinance and cash out to invest in your next property.

CHAPTER EIGHT

HOW TO BOOST YOUR BORROWING POWER – ANOTHER SECRET THE BANKS WON'T LET YOU KNOW

The number one roadblock for property investors preventing them from continuing to invest in the property market is borrowing power restrictions. They simply cannot borrow more!!! Even if they feel comfortable with the new repayment, and they have enough equity or savings, and they spot another great opportunity to invest in again, the banks won't let them!! As an investor who aims to retire with rent, you must understand the lenders' secret formula on how they assess our borrowing power, and how we should reserve and grow our borrowing power for future investment purposes.

Again, there are so many different tactics and strategies for how to boost your borrowing power. For the purpose of this chapter, I will combine them for you, and outline the basic principles. The secret details, of course, will not be disclosed in this book, though you can Google a customised plan for yourself. It is not that I do not want to tell you, it is simply that there is too much information and each person's case is unique. Policies change all the time, and they are not public information either.

However, I have never been stingy with my knowledge. That's why I will introduce a comprehensive and holistic framework below for you to consider what is relevant. And more research and consultation with your own brokers and bankers can take you even further.

First of all, let's go back to the fundamentals of 'The Five C's of Credit'. It is a key principle of measuring a borrower's capacity to repay the loan both in qualitative and quantitative factors. More simply, this means:

1. Capacity: Debt to Income Ratio - if the bank's policy is 1:6, it means that if you earn $100,000 gross annual salary, you can borrow roughly $600,000 loan amount, give or take. Each bank has a different matrix, which we will unfold in detail in this chapter.

2. Capital: How much saving the borrower will contribute towards the purchase. A relevant terminology is Loan to Value Ratio (LVR). If the banks lend you 80% of the purchase price, it means you need to prepare 20% plus

stamp duty and other costs as the minimum deposit required, to show the banks that you are ready.

3. Collateral: This also means 'security' - if you default your repayment for a period of time, the banks have the right to sell it off and take the loan back.

4. Character: In most cases, the lenders look at credit history over the past seven years. If you have defaults or late payment history, it will largely affect your chance to get a low-cost mortgage. Sometimes it may also affect your borrowing power if you must pay higher than average market rate.

5. Conditions: Each borrower may have different circumstances and requirements. For example, most lenders do not accept display homes as security, and for those who do accept them, they also require principal and interest repayment. Different examples can be endless.

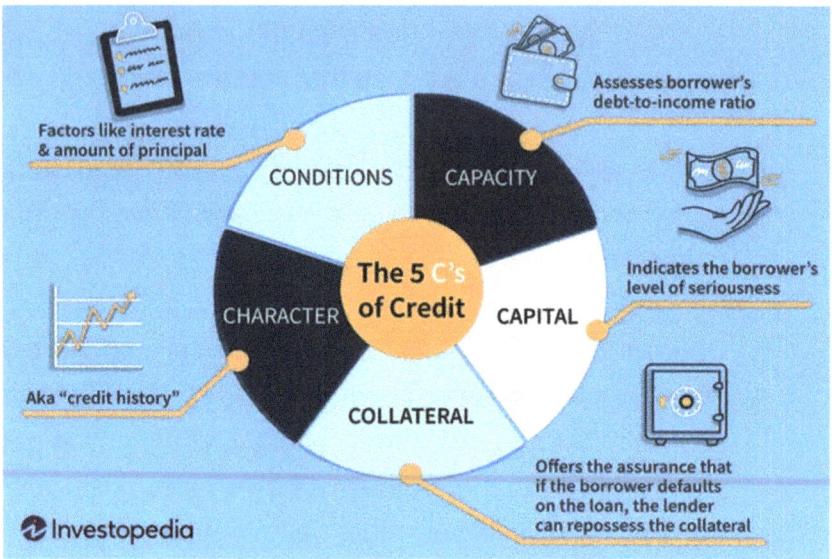

(Reference: Investopedia)

Secondly, the banks can use different formulas and variables for their own risk mitigation. Most banks are very similar when it comes to residential mortgages. The most popular formula is called the 'Net Surplus Ratio' formula, which is outlined below:

- Net income after tax
- Minus basic living expense
- Minus all financial commitments
- The result has to be passing $1 to $200 or more.

Many online articles tell you bits and pieces, without telling you the fundamentals and principle, which will allow you to do your own deep thinking.

How To Boost Your Borrowing Power

Let's break down the secret formula in more detail. Each lender is different when it comes to their policies. This indicates their funding cost and risk appetite. Here is an internal cheat sheet that I prepared to coach many mortgage brokers to break through the borrowing capacity competition.

Now, let's be a reverse engineer, starting from the end goal, so we can learn to think like a bank.

Variable on the formula	Questions you need to ask	Tips to increase borrowing power
Decode: What is included in net income after tax?		
Your PAYG salary income	Do the banks take a one-day employee policy? Do they require three months or six months or twelve months minimum employment history?	Choose the lenders that accept your circumstance, such as probation period, short employment history. Many smaller lenders are more conservative these days, requiring six months or longer employment history with the same employer. However, this also means that stability with your employment or income position will enhance your application.
Your overtime and bonus	Do they accept 100% of my overtime income and bonus to service my loan? Or 80%? Most banks are conservative, and won't believe you will work overtime and receive the bonus every year, so they usually ask for two years average or take the lower year, and also shadow 20% off to feel more comfortable.	This is of course unfair to some special industries, such as health and emergency work, for whom overtime is very normal. Choose the banks that can accept it 100% rather than 80%. It is also not fair to those high performing sales professionals to take the lower year out of the two if their constant wage increase is foreseeable. Hence why I say research is important, rather than just using your everyday bank for your mortgage.
Salary sacrifice	What percentage of salary sacrifice do they take to service my loan?	Most banks understand salary sacrifice arrangements and its tax advantage. But unfortunately, some banks double count the tax and reduce the borrowing power significantly. Avoid those.

How To Boost Your Borrowing Power

Variable on the formula	Questions you need to ask	Tips to increase borrowing power
Your current rental income	Do they take 50%, 80% or 100% of my rental income to service my loan? Most banks take 80% of the rental income to service the loan in case of some economic factors which may cause the rental to drop, such as COV-19 impacting CBD rent for two years, or oversupply in future. In some high vacancy areas the banks will take a higher discount on the actual rental. So, it will disadvantage your borrowing power.	Try to use the banks that take 80% - 100% of the rental income who have confidence in your choice of properties as well. However, it is also wise to listen to many banks' opinions. If many banks use less than 80% rental income for that suburb, it may already indicate an oversupply coming up. They see a lot of upcoming new development two to three years in advance, and they also forecast the population growth in the local area. Hence why some banks may predict there will be a rental drop for those areas.

Variable on the formula	Questions you need to ask	Tips to increase borrowing power
Your future rental income	Some banks will ask for evidence to prove you will rent out some of the vacant property, such as during the tenancy change period, or you just move out from a property and plan to rent it out but not yet secure a tenant. But some banks can simply take a rental appraisal from the property management agent and trust their clients and the market.	Many clients feel shy about asking their brokers and bankers how they come up with the borrowing power results. I would encourage you to challenge or at least ask them to explain why it is what it is. It is a great learning process and maybe sometimes you will come up with a method to increase the borrowing power yourself. At least give yourself the opportunity to discuss. Why do I want to say that? What if your banker did not tell you that he or she cannot use your rental appraisal income? But the banker next door can use that potential rental income of a property yet to be rented out, which results in 120k extra borrowing power.

How To Boost Your Borrowing Power

Variable on the formula	Questions you need to ask	Tips to increase borrowing power
What about Airbnb income?	It is getting very popular and widely accepted by banks now given that many Airbnb hosts have more than two years tax return on the rental income from Airbnb. Some can take 60%, some can take 80%.	Research! Research! Research! Use brokers who are good at research!! Being loyal to a bank does not help you to retire early. Don't be too nice by accepting whatever is recommended by your brokers. Many lazy brokers do big fours only. You can do it better by going to a shopping centre with more than four banks' branches. Again, ask, what income they considered, and how they used it in the calculator? Ask how you can work together to improve it?

Variable on the formula	Questions you need to ask	Tips to increase borrowing power
Your investment income	Usually, the banks accept two years average or the lower out of the past two years investment income from trading shares and receiving dividends or interests. However, many banks are still too afraid to accept crypto trading income. There are only a few who have started doing so. Capital gain income cannot be accepted as usually most people cannot prove they sell one property every year for 30 years.	Plan ahead with your accountant; if you boost your tax return it will help with your new purchase plan.
Your non-taxable income	Government pension, age pension, army reserve income, etc. There are many small incomes can be included that not many people think of.	Maybe I should encourage you to join the army reserve.

How To Boost Your Borrowing Power

Variable on the formula	Questions you need to ask	Tips to increase borrowing power
Consider a longer loan term	Most banks will use a 30-year loan term to service the loan. They will assume you will use 30 years maximum to repay. However, some banks can also use 40 years for first home buyers. And on the other hand, for some people who are above 55, some banks may not give them a 30-year loan term, whereas other banks do.	Research is important because not many brokers know which bank will offer 40 years for first home buyers which will boost a lot of their borrowing power to enable them to buy a property earlier. Not many brokers know how to convince the lenders to give a 30-year mortgage loan term as well for people above 55. It is crucial to find a good broker.
For self-employed and entrepreneurs, business income	It is very complicated to decode how the banks understand self-employed income and entrepreneurs. Many people may see their business thriving with constant growth, but to many banks, it is also a risk - 'what if' it is not sustainable.	Having a good accountant that also understands mortgage is important. Most accountants don't. They only focus on ATO and tax. Having a good banker or broker that understands tax and self-employed documents, how to interpret and look outside the square for you, is imperative. Plan at least one year ahead. Bring your BAS and draft tax return to your banker and broker to discuss first before you lodge it formally.

Variable on the formula	Questions you need to ask	Tips to increase borrowing power
	Decode: What's included in basic living expenses?	
General living expense (Please see the three inserted reference images below)	How do the banks verify it? Some banks need to see three months of bank statements, others need to see six months or 12 months. Some banks need to see a 12-month bank statement from all your bank accounts and credit card accounts. Some banks and non-banks will trust your own budget tools and estimations. Many lenders will use a benchmark called HEM (Household Expense Measurement). Usually the HEM is from the ABS (Australian Bureau of Statistics). However funnily	It will make a vast difference to use alternative methods and benchmarks to measure someone's living expense and result in a bigger range of borrowing power. It is also about reviewing your own real budget, saving money, and controlling spending to prepare for a growing financial commitment. Do not just simply skip the game, and over-commit to a loan that is beyond your control.

How To Boost Your Borrowing Power

Variable on the formula	Questions you need to ask	Tips to increase borrowing power
	enough, some banks come up with their own HEM that is less friendly to the borrowers. Who would you choose? Decode: What's included in the financial commitments?	
Current home loan repayment	How will the banks look at my current home loan repayment? For example, if your actual repayment is 3% and $5,000 principal and interest a month, some banks may use a 5.5% future rate as a stress test, while others may use actual repayment. The remaining loan term will also affect the repayment.	Your current mortgage repayment will affect your borrowing power. If you can lower the current home loan rate, it will reduce the current loan repayment and hence increase your borrowing power. Of course, if the banks use lower stress tests it will favour your borrowing power. Refinancing and extending the existing loan term will also increase your borrowing power, but as a result, the total interest over the loan term will also be increased.

Variable on the formula	Questions you need to ask	Tips to increase borrowing power
Credit card	The banks usually use 3.8% of your total limit as a minimum monthly repayment even if you always paid off in time without delay.	In the past, some people used AMEX charge cards without limit, but now the banks are getting more and more strict on this. They will capture this information on the comprehensive credit reports. Personally, I recommend lowering the credit limit. Most of us will not even reach the limit but it is reducing our borrowing power. Having a $5,000 limit is more than enough for most people's monthly expenses, but usually the credit card company will give you a $15,000 to $30,000 limit or more. That is more than necessary and encourages overspending. I cut all my credit cards at once before I was applying for a big home loan. For self-employed, you can open a business credit card and it will not count under your personal liabilities.

How To Boost Your Borrowing Power

Variable on the formula	Questions you need to ask	Tips to increase borrowing power
Car loan or lease	This is also considered a financial commitment. If you are an employee, sometimes a 'staff benefit', such as taking out a company car and paying the lease, will largely damage your borrowing power. It may have some tax benefits, but remember you are still signing up for a 5-7-year car loan, so it will impact your property investment plan for at least 5-7 years.	Unfortunately, most people take out a car loan via a car loan broker only, who does not do home loans and does not have any knowledge in property lending pre-planning. Their job is solely to assist the car sales manager to sell you the car on the day. They will tell you that the repayment is affordable, but they do not fully disclose the interest rate, total costs, or the trick about balloons. Balloon is a term to do with car loans. It applies when you pay the interest for the whole limit, and balloon is the payout figure but cannot be paid down as well. It reduces the repayment per month but increases the total interest cost. For example, having a car loan that is at $100,000 limit, and having a 40% balloon means you need to pay $100,000 x 8% interest. But repayment is only principal and interest for 60% over the loan term of five years. It means that you pay the interest for the 40% balloon as well on top of the p & i for the 60%. For most PAYG workers, I will say that car loans really do not provide much benefit overall.

Variable on the formula	Questions you need to ask	Tips to increase borrowing power
HELP loan/HECS loan	The banks look at HELP/HECS as a personal loan with repayment according to your pay scale and personal tax level. The higher your income is, the more you pay.	There is no interest on the HELP loan. It is smart to take advantage of this and just pay it as normal, even though it reduces some of your borrowing power. However, if it is necessary, and you do have surplus savings, you can also choose to pay it off and borrow more from the bank. But on the banks' loan, you do pay interest. Sometimes people want to borrow more because they want to purchase a larger sized property to occupy.
Proposed home loan repayment term and conditions	The proposed loan's interest rate, loan product, repayment amount per month, repayment type in interest only or principal and interest, loan amount, and term (how many years) will all affect borrowing power.	Again, each choice may only impact your loan amount by 20k to 50k, but if it all adds up, it may result in almost 100k or more. Ensure your mortgage broker is working hard for you. I know that many other books in Australia recommend using an offset account for your home loan, but it may not necessarily be the most practical and value for money option today.

How To Boost Your Borrowing Power

Variable on the formula	Questions you need to ask	Tips to increase borrowing power
	For example, most banks have lower assessment rates on base home loan, and higher assessment rates on package loans with offset accounts. Assessment rate is what the banks predict the future rate may be and they will do a stress test to see if lending this amount to you is viable. Some banks tend to put an assessment rate higher on a loan with an offset account.

Some banks prefer you to have an interest-only loan and will give you a greater loan amount if you choose interest-only repayment. But some banks prefer you to choose principal and interest repayment. | Why?

Many base loans without an offset account will also provide a free redraw facility. This functionally is very similar and achieves the same interest saving result. Some of them cannot be split into separate accounts. And base loans usually do not charge an annual fee of $120 to $400. For many households who do not have more than $100,000 extra saving, technically there is not much benefit to choose an offset account. People can still use the loan account and redraw facility itself to achieve a similar advantage and enjoy lower rates and lower fees. |

Variable on the formula	Questions you need to ask	Tips to increase borrowing power
Surplus	It must be $1 or $200 more. It really depends on the banks' lending appetite, culture in their credit team, the assessor's personal opinion, and overall strength of the deal.	How can you best prepare for this? You need to ensure that you have a clean credit history report, and prepare all documents required by the brokers or bankers to assist them to best propose your application to the assessor and the bank. This will give the assessor more confidence to approve your deal than others who are less prepared. Believe it or not, sometimes when someone is more prepared, the credit team in the bank are willing to support the case more.
DTI (Debt to Income Ratio) If you earn a $100,000 gross salary, you can borrow $600,000 loan amount based on a 1:6 ratio.	1:6 1:7 Or more	The big fours nowadays use 1:7 and they can support the highest lending amount assuming the income is the same. Some other non-banks will do the same as well. However, the low rate and online banks are usually more conservative - they use 1:6 DTI ratio. There are instances where you can go above 1:7 ratio if you show strong income growth and asset level.

How To Boost Your Borrowing Power

Variable on the formula	Questions you need to ask	Tips to increase borrowing power
LVR (Loan to Value ratio)	The bank may offer different LVR to different property types and postcodes.	For those property investors who love to invest in regional areas, commercial property, or special property types, double check the LVR restriction from different lenders to avoid disappointment. Otherwise, even if you have a strong surplus income position, you may still be restricted on the borrowing amount. Another idea is to perhaps avoid fighting with the banks' general policies. Invest with banks who would love to give you high LVR. It may mean you have less risk as well.

Retire On Rent

Below is a breakdown of living expense items, as it's performed by one of the banks, just to demonstrate how detailed it needs to be.

1. Primary Residence
2. Telephone, internet, Pay TV and media streaming subscriptions
3. Transport
4. Groceries
5. Clothing & Personal Care
6. Recreation and Entertainment
7. Public or Government Primary and Secondary Education
8. Higher education and vocational training
9. Childcare
10. Medical & Health
11. General Insurance
12. Other Insurances
13. Other
14. Land tax and body corporate fees on owner occupied principal place of residence
15. Private schooling and tuition
16. Child Maintenance
17. Personal Insurance
18. Investment Property Costs
19. Secondary Residence
20. Rent

GENERAL LIVING AND ENTERTAINMENT EXPENSES

These expense categories will be introduced in AOL.

EXPENSE CATEGORY	DESCRIPTION
Primary Residence Costs (excluding insurance)	Includes home maintenance and repairs, electricity, gas, water, garden maintenance, council rates, housekeeper, other
Telephone, Internet, Pay TV & Media Streaming Subscriptions	Includes landline, internet, mobile phone, subscription services (e.g. Foxtel), other
Transport	Includes, vehicle registration, fuel, vehicle maintenance, roadside assist, parking & tolls, public transport, taxi/ ride-sharing services, vehicle rentals/car-sharing services, other
Groceries	Includes, grocery shopping including alcohol, restaurants and cafes, takeaway/delivery, other
Clothing & Personal Care	Includes clothes & shoes, hair & beauty, other
Recreation and Entertainment	Includes lifestyle and culture, newspapers/magazines/books, sports, hobbies, memberships (gym, fitness courses), gifts, holidays & airfares, donations, other
Public or Government Primary & Secondary Education	Includes other school fees (excl. private/non-government school fees), school uniform, school books, transport to school, school excursions and camps, after-school activities, other dependent costs
Higher Education & Vocational Training (excluding HECS/HELP)	Self-education/professional development, pets, other
Childcare	Childcare/pre-school/kinder, babysitting/nanny/au-pair
Medical & Health (excluding Health Insurance)	Includes doctor, pharmacy, dentist, optical, physio/remedial/chiro/alternative therapies, other
General Insurance (Including Home & Contents on Primary O/Occ Residence)	Includes income protection insurance, business insurance, building/home/contents insurance, vehicle insurance, travel Insurance, ambulance cover, health insurance.
Other Insurances	Other insurance not captured elsewhere
Other Regular and Recurring Expenses	Unique items not covered in above categories (must be explained further).

ADDITIONAL EXPENSES

These expense categories will be introduced in AOL.

EXPENSE CATEGORY	DESCRIPTION
O/Occ Strata, Body Corporate, Land Tax	Strata Fees /Body Corporate Fees (for owner occupied/primary residence excluding investment property)
Private/non government school fees	Private/non government school fees (includes school, tuition and sport fees for private schooling)
Child & Spouse Maintenance	Child support/maintenance payments
Personal Insurance (Life, Health, Sickness and Personal Accident)	Life/accident/Illness Insurance (excluding insurances captured under general insurance, other insurance and those held in Superannuation).
Investment Property Costs (including insurance)	Home maintenance and repairs; Land tax/body corporate/Strata Fees; Building/Home/Contents Insurance; Garden maintenance; Property Management; Landlord insurance; Council rates; Housekeeper; Investment Utilities; Other
Secondary Residence and Holiday home costs (including insurance)	Housing and property expenses on secondary residence including rates, taxes, levies, body corporate and strata fees, repairs and maintenance, other household items and utilities (excluding insurance, telephone, internet and pay TV as they are categorised separately).
Rent	Rent/board if continuing post loan

(Reference: living expense guide from one of the banks, most banks are very similar and need to cover the living expenses comprehensively to comply with ''responsible lending'' guidelines. AOL means 'Apply Online')

How To Boost Your Borrowing Power

Other tips

1) Use a knowledgeable broker who is results-driven and good at research

Find a broker that knows the lenders' policies. I have to say nowadays the mortgage broker award ranking system is designed for the banks and lenders, not in the best interests of the property investors. It is measured by the loan amount that the brokers distributed for the banks, not on the diversification of the lenders they use for the clients. As a result, many top brokers just become a sausage factory - they pick particular vanilla clients, and work with four or five banks or less. They say no to all complicated deals, have different administrative staff in different processes, and lack personalised strategy and navigation for your property portfolio growth. It is about their numbers - you are just a number to them, not a member.

In one of the chapters of his book 'Australian Property Finance Made Simple', Konrad Bobilak discussed in detail the criteria you should use to choose your mortgage broker. These include that the broker should know more than ten lenders' policies inside out, be familiar with trust structure loan, be a property portfolio investor as well, etc. I use his criteria as guidance for my self-development as a mortgage broker as I find it very helpful. It would be a very lucky property investor who finds a broker that fits all criteria. It is very hard, but these criteria also became my training standards for all the new brokers in my company today as well.

At the end of the day, you do not want your mortgage broker or banker to say, 'You have great income and savings, but you cannot borrow for your next investment property anymore'.

2) For self-employed investors, consider low docs
Some self-employed investors have great sales volume and cash flow which may not be reflected on their tax return, but they still have the ability to repay the proposed mortgage; some lenders are willing to support the loan but with a higher interest rate.

Business has ups and downs and investing in property is another business itself. So many business owners still choose to borrow with low docs policies and higher rates, and when their business recovers or does much better on tax return paperwork, they then refinance to lower rate banks.

3) Learn to invest in commercial property
It is hard to avoid the conversation with residential lending managers and residential brokers which begins with, 'Sorry you cannot borrow anymore'.

With great savings and equity position, however, you can. With commercial property with a long-term lease tenant, the banks are usually willing to lend on 50% to 70% without assessing your personal income level too much. We call that 'stand-alone lease docs commercial loan'.

This is the formula for commercial lease docs loan, called Interest Cover Ratio (ICR). If the net rent per year for a dental clinic shop is $100,000 per year, if ICR is 1:2 in one of the banks for this type of tenant background, then it means the banks will take

$100,000/2 which is $50,000 to service the interest repayment, and the other half will remain as your gross rental revenue.

If the current commercial interest rate is 3%, for example, then $50,000/3% is approx. $1,666,666.00. This means that the bank is willing to lend on $1.6 million for this dental clinic within the right LVR.

The commercial property is usually purchased under a trust with a trustee company. And all your other personal liabilities can be 'ignored' provided the tenancy can service your commercial loan repayment.

4) Invest under SMSF

Another advantage under SMSF loan investment, is that it ignores all your other personal liabilities as well. The income they use under the SMSF lending policies is your contribution towards your SMSF and rental income from the SMSF property.

5) Development project investment with pre-sales

Development finance is another type of lending that does not consider your personal income. The debt is serviced by future sales that are committed with a 10% deposit today.

I will have another chapter about commercial lending both in lease docs and development finance in more detail.

It is just like the Monopoly board game. At the beginning people buy residential property, while at the later stage of the game, people buy commercial property and get into property development to win.

CHAPTER NINE

WHAT IS YOUR ENDGAME?

'What is your endgame?' I once asked my mentor in property development.

'Own a few shopping centres,' he replied jokingly.

Of course, earning money is not the ultimate goal for our lives. It is more of a measurement of mastery in our profession. We won't use all of the money we earn, and we can donate it to make the changes we want to see.

Just as he implies, commercial property and development are the most difficult games in property investment. It is such a niche market - it is not small, but is less for individual mum and dad investors and more for professional property investors, people who work-full time in the property market or are running development as a business.

I am proud to serve a few famous commercial property developers and active commercial property investors. I would also like to give credit to those who invite me to look after the debt structure and transactions for them.

So, what is commercial property? I would say anything that is not residential property or related to multi-dwelling construction can be classified as such. 'Commercial' is like a business, that is the whole point. You do not have to be a multi-billionaire to start to invest in commercial property. You only need to be a normal property investor to start from a low-price, entry level one.

There are many benefits to investing in commercial property, so let's take a look at some of them.

1. Positive cashflow is a given
The reasons most commercial properties with a proper tenant and lease agreement will give you positive cashflow is the credit given to the lending policies.

In commercial lending policies, we use the lending formula called ICR (interest cover ratio). Say the net rent is $50,000 p.a., and assuming ICR is 1:2, which means that the banks want to joint venture with you to invest in this property, and half of the rent will be shared with the bank to pay its interest, while the other half of the rent goes to you to pay lease manager, land tax, income tax, etc.

What Is Your Endgame?

Then half of the rent, which is $25,000, will be paying an interest of 3.00% on an interest-only term (assumption), then the loan amount is approx. $830,000.00. Then of course, your rental income after interest, tax and other fees, are most likely to be positive.

Although commercial property loans usually allow lower LVR - not 80%, but mostly 50% to 65% - it gives the landlord less gearing pressure through the economic cycle.

2. Break through the lending limit in residential lending policies

This is also one of the most popular reasons why many professional property investors get into commercial property investment. Simply, they could not borrow anymore to grow their residential property portfolio. While they still had enough savings or equity from their existing portfolio they refinanced and cashed out.

The prerequisite is to purchase the commercial property under a corporate trustee structure. Usually this is a family trust with a company as a trustee.

It is usually called a 'stand-alone' mortgage, which means the mortgage is serviced by the asset's own income and does not require the borrower's personal or business income to service the loan.

So long as you can produce the savings and equity, and buy a commercial property with a long-term lease, or a development project with pre-sale, the banks can lend you the rest without considering your income. You then can borrow forever non-stop.

3. Stability and consistent income (long-term lease)

With residential property, usually the tenant is on a one-year lease term, which is renewable every year. Usually the tenants are young individuals or young families, who are often on the move. Some of them may not necessarily have a strong financial background.

With commercial property, it is usually a much longer term and with a couple of 'options'. For example, this could be a lease term of three years plus two options after the first three years, with each option being a three-year term as well, so we call it a 3 + 3 + 3, making it a nine-year total lease term. Sometimes it can be 5 + 5 + 5 for mature businesses or medium-sized businesses, or even 10 + 10 + 10 for public-listed companies or government offices. And you are dealing with more sophisticated background tenants, who are usually entrepreneurs or business owners and less likely to default on their payment.

Usually, they also come in to invest a lot of money in the renovation to fit into their needs, and are likely to spend anywhere from $50,000 to $300,000 or even more. As a result, it's less likely they will move easily. As a tenant, you can easily enjoy the capital uplift by their input in the renovation (with some rental deduction benefits) and stable long-term rental income.

What Is Your Endgame?

4. High rental yield
The rental growth for a commercial lease is usually higher than for a residential lease - at a fixed rate of 3% to 5% growth p.a. Also, there is less competition in this area. It is easier to build new townhouses and apartments, but harder to build a new commercial property or get a permit for it.

In a capital city - not in its CBD but in the metropole suburbs – for the rental yield as of today, in the 2021 to 2022 financial year, you are looking at circa 4% to 5%. In the outer suburbs, you are looking at between 6% to 10%.

5. Outgoings are paid by the tenants
All the water, electricity, body corporate fees, and council fees are paid by the tenants, so most landlords only need to pay the lease management fee, mortgage interest and land tax. This is in contrast to residential property, for which the landlord usually needs to pay for the water rate, council rate, and body corporate fees as additional costs.

6. High capital growth potential
Commercial property also comes with great potential in capital growth. On average, every 5,000 family households will need a supermarket, a couple of coffee shops, a dry cleaners, a local gym, a barbershop, a few restaurants, a local GP, a local dentist, a few local office suites, etc.

Once the local suburb population grows, and income level grows, a lot of them actually want to stay within the same suburbs or nearby, with all their friends and family they are used to having around. As a result, we see a lot of younger people willing to move into local townhouses or apartments.

All these factors will also push up the local demand for commercial space again. Urbanisation trends are giving commercial property a lot of opportunities nowadays.

There is an upside in development opportunities. You probably drive past a lot of local shopping strips and see a few retail shops being bought out and combined into one new multi-level new building.

I guess you have also guessed that 'knowing how' to get the planning and permit is another way to earn a lot of money in property investment.

7. Run your business like McDonalds
For business owners and entrepreneurs, I really want to emphasise that if one day you can own your own office, your own retail shop, or your own warehouse, and you become your own landlord and have a mature and stable business paying for your own rent, it is another level of business success.

It is like running your business as a McDonalds. There is a McDonalds property team who always pick the right location, and there is a McDonalds restaurant who always pay their rent on time. They enjoy both the business profit, rental income and capital growth in the property value.

You are your own tenant, you know your business inside out, and since you work so hard and make your business successful, why always make other landlords rich but not yourself? On average, the rental cost is 15% to 30% of the rent, depending on the industry and location. During different business cycles or economic cycles, many businesses are killed by its rent. So why not try to own your own business premises yourself after years in the business? It at least makes your business less risky in the long-term if you have control of your own rent.

8. Diversification in property portfolio
I have seen many investors just invest in apartments, or just invest in townhouses, or just invest in second-hand properties. There are of course benefits in all different property types. However, if you want your property portfolio to have more overall stable and balanced growth, and not miss out on either cash flow growth or capital growth, considering adding one more commercial property into your portfolio is not a bad option.

9. Ability to invest collectively
As mentioned above, when investing in commercial property both in lease docs or development sites, most lenders won't consider your income. Therefore, it is more feasible to co-invest a commercial property with your friends and family relatives, or business partners, rather than investing in residential property. For residential property loans, banks need to consider all family household's finances, and how that will affect each other's borrowing as well, so it makes it very complicated, and sometimes impossible to move on.

However, investing in commercial property makes it easier. It is usually under a unit trust with fixed unit shareholders, and the loan is serviced by the lease or pre-sales for development site, so there is no need to assess applicants' different family households' income.

10. Generation of wealth

Commercial property in a premier location and with a long-term lease is one of the most popular choices for many wealthy families to pass on their assets to their children. There are many factors to consider when going down this path, such as long-term lease opportunity - each tenant will commit anywhere from nine years to thirty years. Each generation only needs to handle a few tenants' turnover rather than more than 50 residential tenants turnover.

Usually, the first generation who owns the commercial property will pay off the mortgage. That means that from the second generation onwards, it will be a strong positive cash flow income cash cow.

Unlike most countries, Australia does not have an inheritance tax. So, when you pass it on to future generations, as long your children and grandchildren are responsible - by having very strict rules around not selling the property and instead using the rental income to give their offspring the best education and healthcare as possible - I think your family will be very powerful for many generations to come. This is a very popular choice for many Jewish and Chinese immigrant families. They are minority groups in Australia, and feel less secure in many ways, such as equal opportunity, political opportunity, social pressure, and prejudice, hence they are more sensitive on the wealth management side.

What Is Your Endgame?

So, what kind of commercial properties are available on the property market? Here are a few things you need to consider when it comes to the type of commercial property that might be more suitable to you:

1. Why am I buying it? Is it for long-term holding for high rental income, without so much worry about the capital growth? Or stable rental income and an expectation of higher capital growth? Or am I buying to re-develop or refurbish in a few years, and rental income today is less important to me.

2. Who is the tenant? Can I manage the tenant relationship well or via a lease manager? Does the tenant have a good reputation? Is the tenant's industry doing well in the current economic landscape? Is the tenant's business in their expansion stage or they are more likely to shrink their office size?

3. For the similar properties nearby, what is the rental per square metre and average rental income? What is their rental yield? What is their sold price in comparison?

4. Are there any nearby new developments coming up as a future competition?

5. What's in the terms and conditions that is favouring the tenants but not favouring the landlord?

6. What is the title type? Freehold, strata? Is there any share wall with the neighbour? Is there any future

development opportunity for this site? If so, what's the cost likely to be and future value likely to be?

Overall, we need to think like the bank to mitigate risks. There are mainly two risks from the above: vacancy risk and re-development risk.

Vacancy risk: If this tenant left, how long will it take me to replace the tenant and receive the same or better rent? What if I cannot achieve it, what is the existing strategy and alternative plan for me?

Re-development risk: What is the risk of not getting the planning and permit I expected given that I have to pay above the market price if it is only for a leasehold investment? (Usually the property agents like to sell the old property in a premium location with the expectation that it can obtain a planning permit.) What are the development costs and risks?

Especially after COV-19, our lifestyle has been dramatically changed. 'Essential service' has become a key word. Whatever did not change during COV-19 will deliver long-term stability – things like childcare, GPs, pharmacists, etc. They did not close even during the pandemic.

The development costs, building materials and labour costs are all rising as well. The industry is going through a big reshuffle and it is becoming extremely difficult for new players to enter and old players to survive.

What Is Your Endgame?

The categories in commercial property (lease docs)

1. Retail shops

(Reference: RealCommercial.com.au)

These are usually the street shop front retail shops, though sometimes they can also be in a shopping centre or office building. They can be used for multiple purposes. I personally like this type of investment, although the online shopping trend and COV-19 have changed the landscape of retail commercial properties. I believe there are opportunities in all changes. We see many old retail stores closed and long-term vacancies for many spaces, but there are strong newcomers. People's demand to go out is always there, and retail shops usually occupy a prime location in a neighbourhood with strong traffic. It might be retail today, but can also be converted to an office, dentist, GP, pharmacist, post office, or even high-rise mixed-use apartments and offices in the future.

For recent years (today is the first half of the year 2022) observation in Victoria, the retail rental yield in the metropole area is between 3% to 4%. The more outer suburbs and regional areas can go up to 5% to 8%. Retail shops are slightly lower than other commercial assets during this period when many retails businesses are struggling and asking for rental relief.

What Is Your Endgame?

2. Office spaces

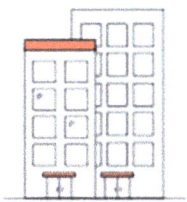

(Reference: RealCommercial.com.au)

Again, office space is being impacted dramatically post COV-19. Many people have become accustomed to working online and working from home. Many businesses have reduced their office space.

Many big companies and big government departments are reducing their office space after COV-19. The pandemic has made them realise that they actually do not need that much office space and are trying to improve the efficiency.

Retire On Rent

Who the tenant is for your office property investment is very important. These factors need to be considered – if the tenant commits to a long-term lease with a penalty for exiting early, and they do leave, how quickly can you replace with a similar tenant?

Is there any renovation cost or incentives to the tenant? This is another thing that needs to be considered. Building renovation costs are usually higher than people expect.

3. Childcare

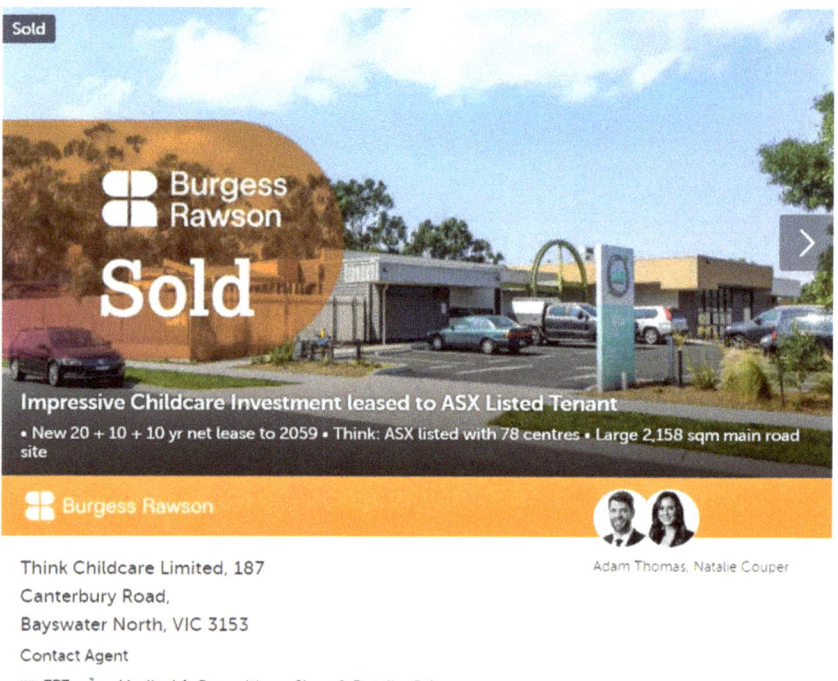

(Reference: RealCommercial.com.au)

What Is Your Endgame?

Childcare is an essential service industry. People need to send their children to school otherwise they cannot go to work properly, and the economy will be largely impacted.

Childcare leases are very stable and long-term; usually they'll be a 30-year lease with stable rental growth per year.

The government is increasing the childcare subsidy and all parties will consistently use it as an election topic. It is certainly a good business and good industry, given the population net growth has been unstoppable in Australia in the past 30 years and will continue to be in the foreseeable future.

I feel a bit of sympathy for many childcare teachers. They are not included in the Teachers' Union, and I wish their pay was higher given the hard work they are providing to our children.

For recent years (today is the first half of the year 2022) observation in Victoria, the rental yield for childcare in the metropole area is anywhere between 4% and 5%. Further suburbs or regions can go up to 6% to 8%.

4. Petrol stations

(Reference: RealCommercial.com.au)

Elon Musk is my idol - the man who made the electric car market a reality. Despite these cars, petrol stations still maintain their investment value.

Firstly, let's look at the argument about when we will abandon the petrol or diesel car totally. Just looking at 'location, location, location', I believe petrol stations still have their advantages. They usually occupy one of the busiest spots in the local area, or a main traffic stop for long distance travel. The land size is usually more than a thousand square metres. It is not uncommon for a petrol station to be converted into a high-rise apartment development, with some extra costs to deal with the contamination of course.

Secondly, many people don't know that the profit for a petrol station business is not just from its petrol, but largely from its

What Is Your Endgame?

retail shop profit, driven by 7/11. Many other brands are trying to adopt this business model as well. Nowadays you will see Woolworths partner up with BP (something they abandoned later on to start their own) and Coles partner up with Shell to complete this business collaboration. Petrol stations are just convenient for many - for those who live nearby, or for those who don't have time to run to the supermarket but need to quickly grab some essential goods from the retail store after they fill up their patrol. Some people believe that when the electricity station replaces the petrol station, the petrol station may still be able to survive.

Thirdly, you will sign up with a very stable and financially strong tenant. Most petrol stations are publicly listed or Global 500, such as Shell (Coles Express), BP, Woolworth Caltex, Caltex (Smart Mart supermarket), 7/11 and Mobile, United 24, Puma, etc. Usually they are financially sound and sign a very long-term lease. Petrol station services were essential services, too, during COV-19.

The discussion about when the technology in electric cars will be mature enough to replace gas is a very interesting one. Some facts presented by The New York Times (data from the U.S.):

- By 2021, fewer than 1% of cars on the road are electric.
- Automakers are now shifting to electric vehicles, which could make up one-quarter of new sales **by 2035**, analysts project. But at that point, **only 13%** of vehicles on the road would be electric. Why? Because older cars can stick around for a decade or two.

- Even **in 2050**, when electric vehicles are projected to make up 60% of new sales, **the majority of vehicles on the road would still run on gasoline.** Slow fleet turnover is a major challenge for climate policy.
- If the United States wanted to move to **a fully electric fleet by 2050** — to meet President Biden's goal of net zero emissions — then sales of gasoline-powered vehicles would likely have to end altogether by around 2035, which would require a significant departure from projections.

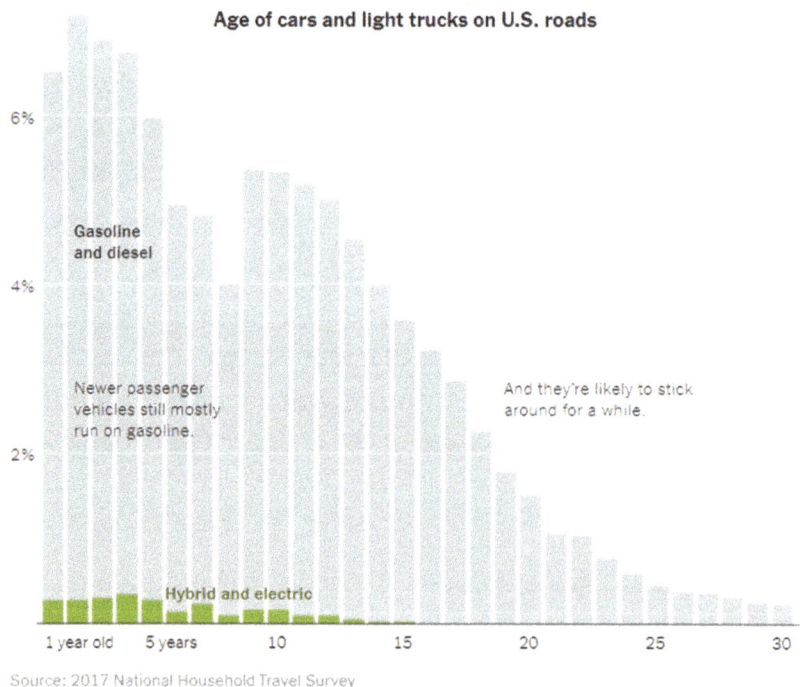

So, it seems like the ideal goal of being gas-free will be around 30 years away. To have a property in a prime location with a

What Is Your Endgame?

good tenant for 30 years before turning it into a development site is the goal of many petrol station investors.

For recent years (today is the first half of the year 2022) observation in Victoria, as an indication, the rental yield for petrol stations near the metropole area but not next to the CBD, will be anywhere between 3%-5% ish p.a. For further suburbs or regionals, this number can go up to 6% to 12%.

5. Health-related assets, such as GP clinics, dental clinics, aged care

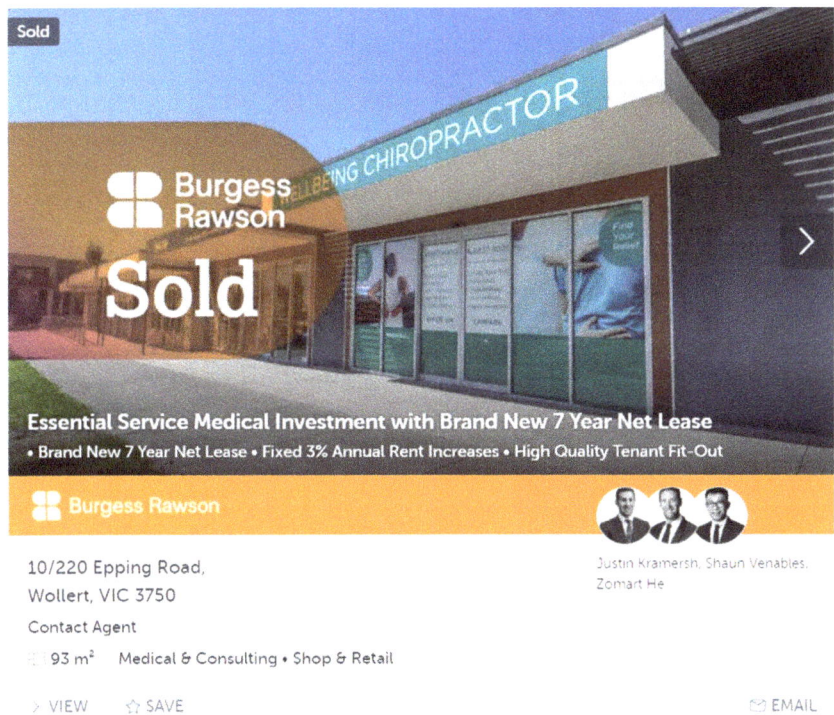

(Reference: RealCommercial.com.au)

As discussed, these were all essential services during COV-19. Although some dental clinic hours were reduced for non-emergency surgery, they were the first ones to re-open with appointments fully booked for a long period of time.

It is lucky to get a GP tenant or dental clinic tenant, because once their business is established, they rarely move. Their clients are very familiar with their location.

Sometimes I also see GPs and dental clinics move to a nearby location because they want to purchase their own places and become their own landlord.

The rental yield for GPs and clinics is similar to the range for retail and offices, from my own observations.

Aged care is perhaps one of the more specialised assets as well. It is usually operated by very professional health care providers - some are public listed companies, some are non-for-profit organisations. It is very difficult for them to relocate because the planning and development permit is extremely difficult to obtain. Plus, the demand is increasing due to the ageing and growing population, but the supply is growing slowly. So, these are very long-term tenants.

The rental yield for aged care is similar to childcare, from my own observations.

What Is Your Endgame?

6. Industry warehouses

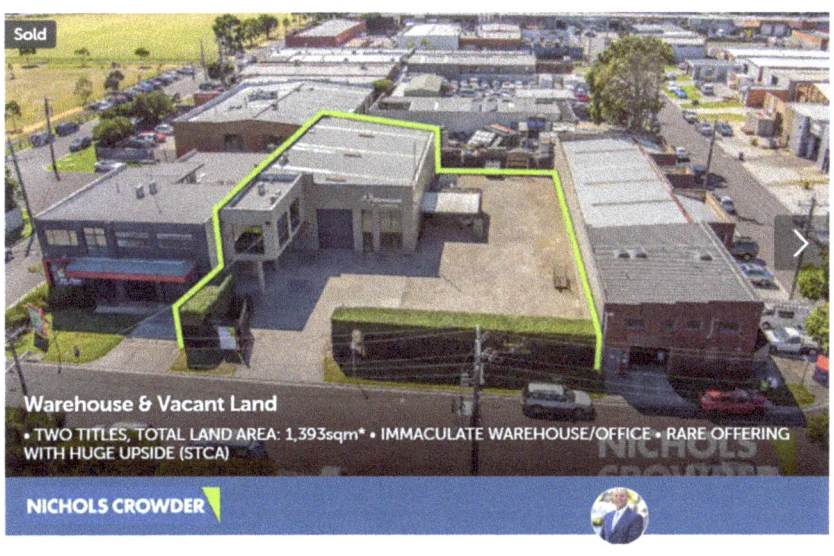

(Reference: RealCommercial.com.au)

Thanks to COV-19, people are adopting the habit of shopping online more than ever before. As a result, the demand for warehouses for e-commerce has increased dramatically. It's quick to build a warehouse, given it is usually a simple structure inside - just like a big box with four walls, and an office suite inside.

Of course, e-commerce is not the only purpose for warehouses. The growth of the economy demands more warehouses for multiple purposes, such as storage, industrial activities, construction industry use, or even funky offices, beer bars and cafes.

What Is Your Endgame?

7. Hotels, motels, pubs, rooming houses, caravan parks etc.

Hotel, Motel, Pub & Leisure

(Reference: RealCommercial.com.au)

One of my objectives is to own and run a hotel-like business. It is a very good cash-cow business model. But of course, I am not there yet. It requires a lot of capital to do so. However, I do co-own a small caravan park and enjoy the benefits and return, even through COV-19.

The banks call these types of assets 'hospitality and tourism'. It is a very interesting and diversified industry. For example, there are different levels of hotels - big international brands such as Novotel, or small local franchise brands such as Quest. Then you have regional motels, or hostels for young tourism. Pubs for drinks, poker machines and also some rooms for travellers, caravan parks for family road trips, and so on.

These all have different target audiences and related economic activities behind it. For example, most big internal brands during COV-19 were largely impacted by the shutdown of international borders, and tourists hesitated to come back immediately like before. As a result, many hotels are actually closing down the business or running at a loss. Some of the 'lucky' ones have been used as government quarantine hotels and earned some temporary rents.

On the other hand, pub and caravan's business profits were happily increasing. People during lockdown were depressed and local pubs were one of the few options they had. Even during lockdown when they could not go to the pub, they could still order alcohol delivery.

What Is Your Endgame?

8. Farm landings

Rural

$1,650,000

, Coldstream

5　3　3　16.19 ha　Acreage

Sold on 07 Sep 2015

(Reference: RealEstate.com.au)

Land is becoming a scarcity in the world of consistently rising populations in Australia. Hence, we are seeing many farmlands near the metropole areas becoming new residential developments. This is also due to the model farming machinery and chemicals that have made agriculture production more efficient, enabling us to produce more food with less labour and less land.

This is giving many long-term property investors a chance to enjoy their capital gains multiplying. What they do is buy multiple acres of land that used to be farmland, but is now most commonly an old residential home. They hold it for five to ten years on average, waiting for it to be re-zoned or for a better chance to subdivide the land. This requires more capital investment at the beginning because they are usually selling for a few million dollars to start with. But it is usually more than 'double in ten years'. Sometimes I see double in three to five years, or three to five times growth in ten years.

I guess 'the rich get richer'.

9. Multi units of apartments or old units

This is a very capital intensive and high-risk commercial development project type as well. It requires a significant skillset and project management experience. It also requires a lot of due diligence before purchasing a site with potential to obtain a development approval or planning and permit for a high-density project.

What Is Your Endgame?

(Reference: medium.com)

(Reference: RightPropertyGroup.com)

It can certainly be very profitable, but unless you are a professional developer or you have a close relationship with a development management team, then I would recommend staying away. I have seen many first-time developers get it wrong.

Of course, it is a smart way and the fastest way to accumulate debt-free properties to develop and keep.

Retire On Rent

If you want to avoid such risk, you can also buy the existing old unit complexes and hold them for the high yield.

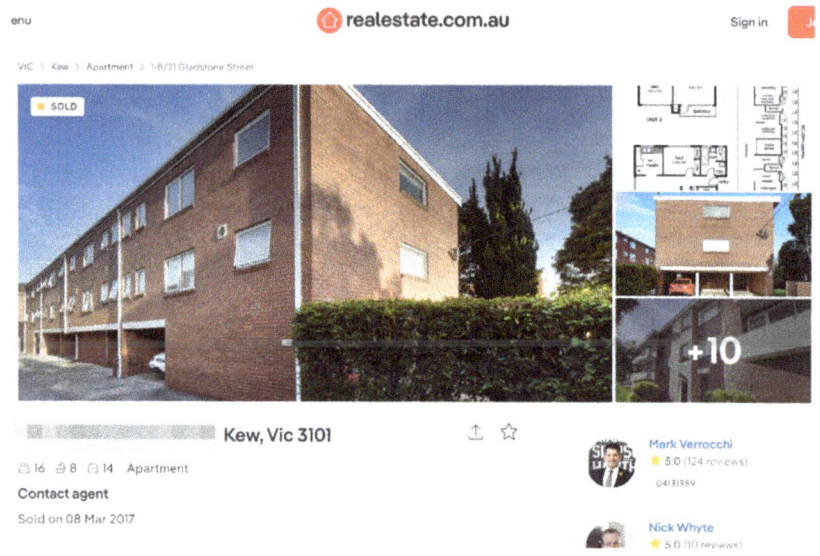

(Reference: RealEstate.com.au)

What Is Your Endgame?

The above example has two bedrooms in each unit with one car spot. The range for Kew's rental (in Victoria) is between $380 to $410 per week for eight units. So, the rental income range for the whole complex is between $158,080 to $170,560. It is a mature and established suburb, so it is relatively easy to rent them out.

10. Build your own Airbnb
Airbnb is the largest hotel in the world. It is giving dedicated and smart people a chance to earn a higher than normal yield. Of course, it takes more time to run it like a business or pass the great location to an Airbnb management company. The good ones I have seen earn 40% more than the market normal rent, sometimes more.

Personally, I often love to stay in Airbnbs while travelling. They are much larger spaces than many hotels, and are more a part of the local communities and environment. You do not feel like a tourist, but more like one of the neighbours.

Unique stays
Spaces that are more than just a place to sleep

(Reference: AirBnB.com)

You cannot simply buy an existing Airbnb site - it is very hard to find one. If it is profitable, most likely the landlord will keep it. And Airbnb is still very new to the market. The banks just started recognising its rental income in loan servicing. But the banks still remain conservative. They ask for two years to prove its consistent rental income and shadow off 40% at least to avoid velocity in the long-term.

There are good hosts and bad hosts. Good locations, ordinary locations. Increasing competition and the changing of the tourism industry landscape. So, it is hard to advise whether it is profitable to run Airbnb to collect rent or not. It really depends on how you are going to run yours.

11. NDIS

NDIS stands for National Disability Insurance Scheme. It has been a very hot topic since 2021 and is getting more and more popular nowadays. The government is beginning to roll out greater support for those who are in need - creating jobs, more carers for the disability participants, and rental income to the NDIS housing providers. The NDIS housing providers then pay the landlord a high fixed rental return with a very long fixed lease, which can sometimes be up to 10 + 10 years.

The reason the rental return is higher than the market price, sometimes double or more, is that the house quality is specifically designed for disability participants, and includes things such as wheelchair access, larger door size, disability toilet, single floor, etc. The building costs are usually higher than normal residential houses per square metre. These may drive lower market resale prices in the future, hence paying a higher than market average price will make it more attractive to the landlord.

However, challenges also arise as it is very new in the market, and market resale price could be lower. Some new settlements suffer a lower than market valuation, around 10%, meaning it is not suitable for high gearing investors.

Watch this space. It is certainly a very interesting increasing niche market. The more we support it, the better it is for the disability participants in our society, and the more jobs created by this market.

Terminology and general ideas for commercial lending lease docs

1. LVR: Usually the commercial lease will generate between 50% and 70% LVR.

2. Loan amount: Different loan amounts may fall into different segments of the lending policies. For example, in one of the big fours, in its commercial department, there are segments for $0 to $300k loan amounts, $300k above to $1 mil, $1 mil to $15 mil, $15 mil to $60 mil, $60 mil and above. You will speak to different lending managers or bankers, and face different risk criteria as well. Different lenders may be good at different segments, hence why it is also worthwhile to have a good commercial broker.

3. ICR (Interest Cover Ratio): This represents the appetite of a lender in terms of how much they like the prospect of the lease and tenants, or the assets. For example, if the interest cover ratio is 2:1 times, it means $200,000 net rent will cover

What Is Your Endgame?

$100,000 interest-only repayment. If the interest rate is at 3%, then the $200,000 rent can service up to approx. $3,300,000 loan amount.

[Formula = $200,000 net rent per year / 2 / 3% = approx. $3,300,000 loan amount]

Then consider the LVR cap, and whichever is lower will be the final loan amount.

If the banks do not like the tenant as much, they will increase the ICR requirements. If they increase the ICR to 3:1, then it means the $200,000 net rental income per year can only service up to an annual interest only repayment of $66,666, which is covering a 3% annual interest rate for a loan amount of $2,200,000 rather than $3.3 mil above.

[Formula = $200,000 net rent per year / 3 / 3% = approx. $2,200,000 loan amount]

4. Loan Term: There is usually a two-to-five-year loan term for many commercial lease docs. Nowadays funding costs mean that the shorter the loan term, the lower the interest rate can be. It is usually no longer than the term of the lease and requires renewal at the end of each tenancy's term, whether they are going to renew or not.

The banks have common sense and are friendly to work with for their customers during the renewal. If the tenant leaves, and it takes sometimes say three-to-six months to find another long-term tenant, the banks will usually still approve you with one extra year for you to find the new tenant, then give a new long-term loan term again. And the banks won't simply ask you to repay all the money at the end of the term.

5. Repayment and amortisation: Most lease docs commercial loans can give you interest-only repayments and renew at the end of every term if a good tenant continues. But doesn't that mean making the interest-only repayment forever?

Or, if the loan term is short, not like a 30-year residential mortgage, how does the borrower repay the principal aside from voluntary repayment?

There is a term called 'amortisation' which relates to commercial lease docs loans. For example, if you get a three-year loan term and it is interest-only, due to higher LVR and higher gearing, sometimes the banks may ask you to reduce 5% of its principal amount every three years and divide evenly in each repayment.

So, giving a specific example, if an office is purchased for $2 million, and the loan amount is 65% which is $1.3 million. The interest-only repayment at 3% p.a. is $39,000. If the bank asks for 5% principal to be repaid in three years, which is $100,000, divided by three years, this is $33,333 principal deduction per year. So, the total repayment per year will be $39,000 + $33,333 = $72,333.33. If the rental yield is at 4.5% x $2,000,000, then the net rent before interest is $90,000. The rent after interest per year is $17,666.67.

6. Renewal and refinance risk, and vacant possession value: Now, there is a risk if it is hard to find a new tenant to replace the previous tenant, especially if the site is too far away and somewhere with low population, or the previous tenant was too large and too specialised. It will usually come with a longer than one-year vacancy period. At this time, the banks may ask you to reduce the LVR to 50% of the new vacancy value, not necessarily to repay the whole loan off.

The commercial property value is very sensitive to its tenancy income. Many commercial agents will avoid mentioning the 'as if vacant possession value' to potential buyers. So, the buyers need to do their own homework. This is a very common concept in property valuation and should be common knowledge for long-term commercial property investors.

For example, government tenants or some public companies like to pay above the market average rental income because they usually have a large space or special design for their building. But once they vacate, it is hard to find a similar tenant to replace the whole space. The landlord then needs to invest a lot of money to subdivide a big space into multiple smaller office areas and receive less rent per square metre. If the rental drops 20% overall, the commercial property value will of course drop 20% or more.

7. Valuation report by a third party: 'The valuer is the eyes and ears for the banks.' This is an old saying in the Property Faculty at university. The banks do not have the time to go out and evaluate each property individually.

By now you probably realise the validity in the commercial tenant's market and how that may negatively impact your cash flow position.

Tenancy profile analysis is what an independent valuer will provide for a very affordable cost prior to your purchase. That is called 'purchaser advice', with fees for service. And if you happen to win on the auction or through a private offer, you then can roll over the report to a bank version valuation report, which is compulsory. So really, you are saving money and mitigating risks. If you don't pay for the due diligence, very likely you will then pay a premium price for the purchase later.

Valuers do not just do tenancy profile analysis, they also do local market rent analysis, economic outlook analysis, etc. More importantly, because the market is small in Australia, all valuers know the other valuers, they graduate from the same schools, maybe used to work in the same firms, they exchange information and market insights. They may help you to avoid getting into some risky deals. For example, if you want to purchase a property with a long-term lease, but there is a possibility that this tenant will leave soon and break the lease term, the agent will not tell you this. However, the valuer who acts as the 'pre-purchase advisor' will.

As a conclusion, commercial property with lease and rental income will help you to break through the serviceability cap and limit. It is one of the best options to help a big family to hold on to wealth generation after generation. All you need is enough deposit or equity, and a strong interest in studying its market.

CHAPTER TEN

COMMERCIAL PROPERTY INVESTMENT (DEVELOPMENT OPPORTUNITIES WITH CAPITAL INCOME) IN A NUTSHELL – THE ENDGAME IN PROPERTY INVESTMENT

Now, welcome to the commercial property world. You may have realised by now that anything that is not normal and not residential is categorised as commercial. These are unique, case-by-case, more complicated, have a higher level of entry and more risk, but are also more profitable.

Developing the property project can be a full-time job, or full-time business. Conversely, some people treat this as a hobby or alternative investment option and have a side project every two or three years.

Again, the advantage is that provided you have enough deposit, you can enter the game. And, for many development types, you will not be required to demonstrate serviceability. Here is a brief introduction to all different property development options.

Categories in property development

1. Duplex development

A duplex is a side-by-side townhouse without a common driveway. It usually has a common wall in the middle. It utilises the land size to build a big and deep two-storey structure.

Below is an example of a property after the duplex is complete (designer impression):

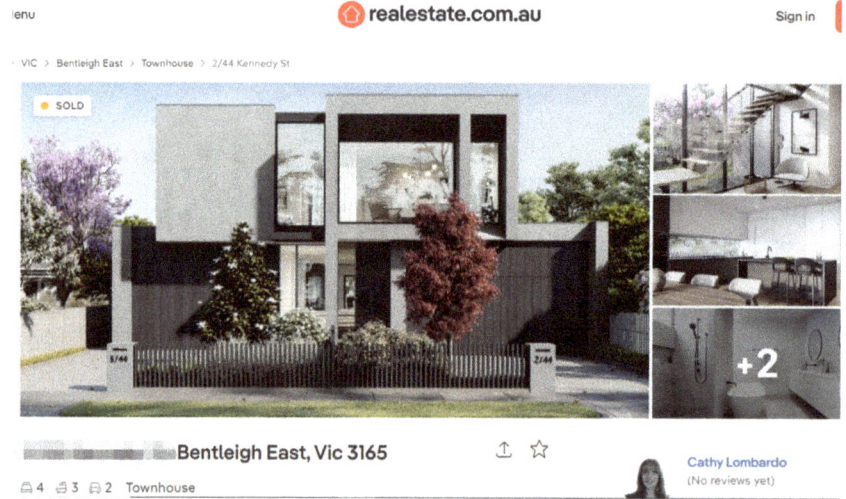

Commercial Property Investment

Commercial Property Investment

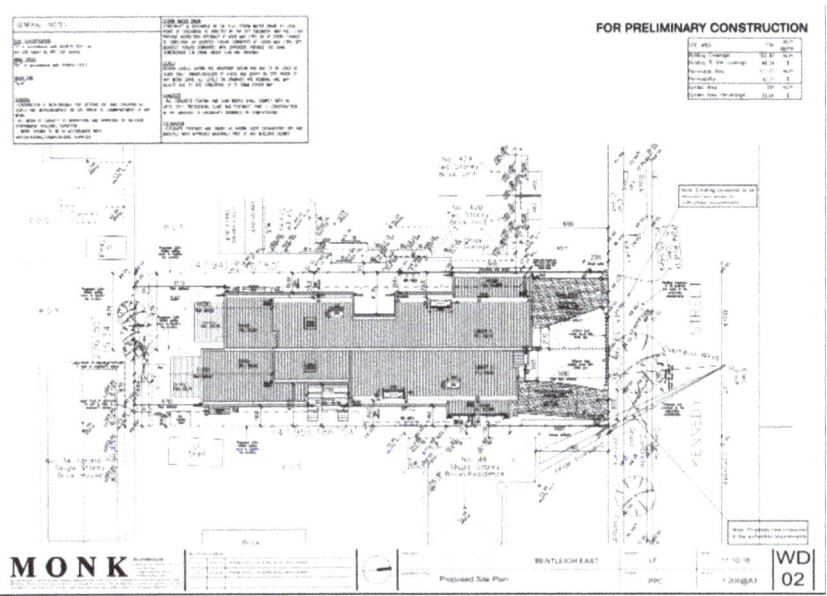

Property (pictured below) before the duplex development:

Commercial Property Investment

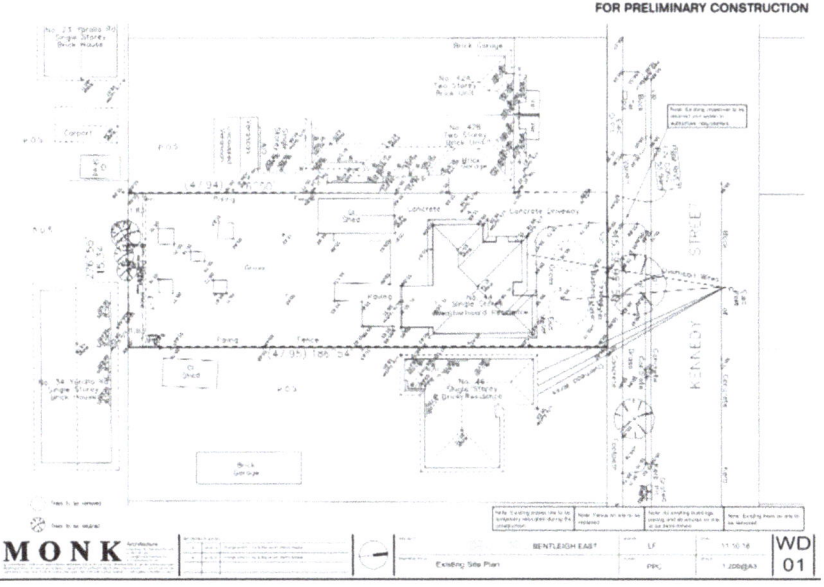

(Reference: RealEstate.com.au)

This beautifully designed duplex was sold into Unit 1 and Unit 2, with four bedrooms each and for two families. The old pictures were before its construction; it was previously an old house with very low rental yield, around $320 to $380 per week. After completion this number was up to $1,000 to $1,200 per week each unit, or $2,000 to $2,400 per week in total. The liveable area is almost double internally with two townhouses rather than one single-storey older house.

So, after the duplex was built, both rental yield opportunity and capital value (due to more liveable area) were increased. This is a great option for those who have high taxable income and are looking for positive cashflow properties, and also come with great value in depreciation.

Newly built property comes with the benefit of depreciation. For example, if a townhouse cost $600,000 to build, and according to the depreciation table, you are losing $30,000 value every year as the build depreciates, then you can claim this $30,000 as a loss against your rental income. If you are eligible for negative gearing, then you may claim tax back from the ATO.

2. Develop the backyard
Although duplex developments can maximise both the capital value and rental yield, they require a lot of cash at the beginning, involve a lot of work in town planning and design, and risks in construction.

Therefore, there are many smart investors buying properties with big backyards and large frontage with enough room to

Commercial Property Investment

build a separate driveway. These will only require a deposit for one new building rather than two. Sometimes if you are patient enough, you can wait for three to five years while the house value goes up, and then you can cash out the increased value and use it as the deposit for the new build in the backyard. So it sounds like $0 down money deal for the unit at the back.

Keeping the original unit at the front will allow its rental income to assist the interest repayment, so that you are not losing rental income during the construction period for something like a duplex development – though you may need to consider some rental deduction due to the noise.

(Reference: The West Australian; An aerial view of a land subdivision for a backyard)

Retire On Rent

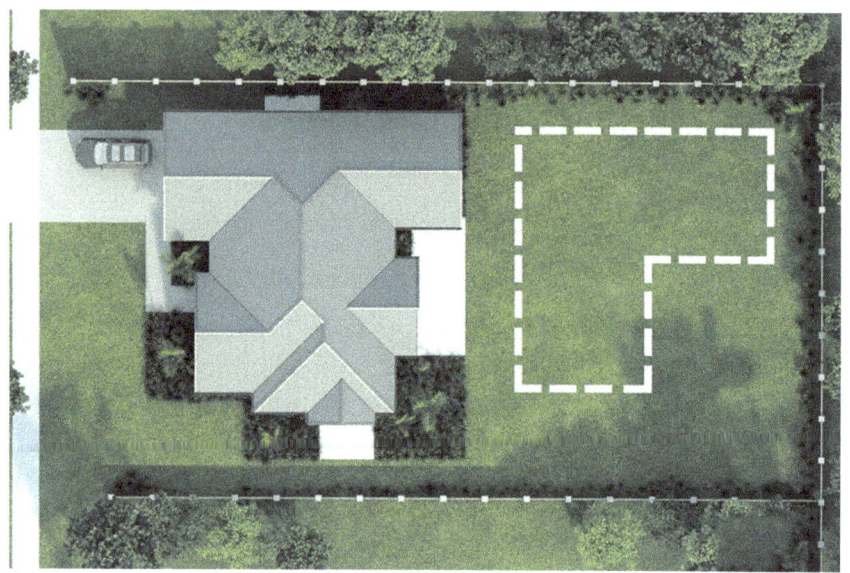

(Reference: LandDividers.co.nz)

3. Multiple units/townhouse developments

Three or four properties will be a tipping point in development finance. If you develop three or four units, or more, many banks' policies then classify you as a developer for this case. They will not use future rental income, and they also will not require your own income to service the land and construction loan. What they then require is for you to sell some of the units as 'off-the-plan' to the market and use the purchasers' 10% deposit as a guarantee for the debt. The lenders will lend you say 70% to 80% of the total development costs (hard costs, including land and build), with capitalised interest repayment during the loan term. And as a developer you need to contribute the equity or cash for the rest of 20% to 30% plus all the interests pre-paid upfront.

Capitalised interest means you pre-paid all the interest.

Many developers actually love this idea and overall policy. It means that if they secure a good potential site for a future multi-unit/townhouse development planning and permit, they have a great opportunity to achieve exceptional profits.

This type of development requires a lot more professional experience and risk.

(Reference: https://www.empiredesigns.com.au/townhouse-developments)

Many builders and developers will build a multi-unit project, sell enough units to achieve the banks' lending requirements, and then keep the rest to make this project 'profit-free'. They then use a residential loan to cash out the units they are keeping (must be less than three or four to keep in the same project). The loan they then take out will occur at interest cost to offset the future rental income as well. The cash out equity is not a taxable income, but they are enjoying the equity they are building for themselves. They can use it for the next project.

'The rich get richer.'

Commercial Property Investment

4. Development in apartments or mixed use

(Reference: University of Delaware)

Commercial Property Investment

I do not want to reinvent the wheel - I am simply summarising all the possible options for the property investors in Australia. The above infographics were contributed by a U.S. university. This property type can be a very small development site, with a cafe or retail on the ground floor, and two or three extra levels above as apartments. You can sell all the apartments and keep the ground floor retail debt-free. Or you can go as large as a 100-land subdivision with a super lot (a super large-sized lot) for a childcare or a retail strip. It will make these small communities more walkable and liveable.

You are probably walking past many of these kinds of examples every day. For example, a small-medium high rise building on the main street, with a cafe downstairs and apartments upstairs would fit into this category. Or in a newly developed area, where there are many new houses built, and many new shopping strips in the middle.

This type of development project is mixing multiple purposes – they are not just residential, but also servicing the needs for the local residents with things such as retail, health, office space, etc.

5. Farmland rezone and multi-unit land subdivision

▲ The planning permit would allow two of the larger properties to be subdivided to make way for about 200 residential lots.

(Reference: The Urban Developer)

Buying large farmland and holding it until the council rezone it for residential purposes can produce a great opportunity to do land subdivision and create more residential lots. There is a high capital uplift once the zoning is changed.

Commercial Property Investment

For example, a big farmland with or without a house on it may only be worth $1 million. Once the council allows and encourages developers to create more residential lots there, it may be worth $3 million. If you obtain a permit for 200 lots, the market value may increase again to $5 million because it now has more certainty for the development profit.

However, in Victoria and NSW, there is a new tax rule which may be introduced soon, called 'The Windfall Tax' from the first of July 2022. We jokingly call it 'The Rich Men Tax'.

(Reference: Farm Online)

This infographic explains it very well. It is basically an extra capital gains tax and cuts off the upper profit of the land value increase. Personally, I think it is unfair to the developers, because under the pressure of population increases and affordable housing, this is discouraging the developers from creating more residential houses for the market.

6. Potential development sites on existing commercial properties

(Reference: Urban.com.au)

This is a famous apartment building in Box Hill, Victoria. Inside it are 438 apartments and multiple levels of retail and office. As you can see, there were many old retail shops around the area. It was sold as a few retail shops next to each other, then acquired by a developer group, who applied for a planning permit to build a high-rise building.

Today we call Box Hill the second CBD in Melbourne. There are a few dozen new high-rise buildings that have been approved and are waiting to be completed.

Commercial Property Investment

You do not have to get into Box Hill to earn a fortune. Australia is into the concept of satellite cities, so there are many suburbs being developed with high rises. Holding the key locations in those suburbs for future opportunities and having expertise in town planning and the long-term vision of the city is the key to success.

Terminology and general ideas for development finance:

1. DCR (Debt Cover Ratio): This means the pre-sales contract value needs to cover the proposed construction loan amount you need from the banks.

2. QPS (Qualified Pre-sales): Not every pre-sale will be recognised by the banks nowadays. For example, some foreign purchasers, or interstate investors, may not necessarily be acceptable, or there will be a limited quota for them.

3. LVR in GRV and TDC: This is a facility limit measured by different measurements. Usually it is GRV (Gross Realisation Value), which is the total of as if completed contract prices. If it is NRV (Net Realisation Value), there is less GST and sales commission. TDC is the Total Development Cost, which is usually the land value plus the build contract value less GST. The lenders will usually take whichever is lower at the end.

4. QS: Quantitative Surveyors will provide an estimation of the contract cost. Just like the valuation report, the QS report is the eyes and ears for the banks. They will need to verify it if the builders' quotes are over-quoted or under-quoted. Both of these are risks to the developer. Of course no one wants to pay too much. However, under-quoting means the builder is likely to ask for more money after the construction starts, and there is a risk of the developer not being able to complete the project if he does not have enough extra funds later, when the construction kick starts.

5. Valuation: Valuation for development finance is a little bit different from lease docs loan. It involves measuring the land value today, and the value with the planning and permit. More importantly, they value it using the 'as if completed' status. What will be the market selling price if the property's construction was completed today, factoring in all the local market competitions and forecast economic outlook.

6. Capitalised interest: This means the construction loan interest for 12 to 24 months or longer, depending on the construction timeframe, will be paid in advance at the beginning of the loan. If the project finishes early though, the extra interest will be repaid.

7. Loan term: Usually land banking loan terms are between 12 and 24 months. 36 months is the maximum because it is leading to construction very soon. For construction, the loan term is equal to the construction period plus a three-month buffer.

8. Builder background: A good lender will verify the builder's background through their own sources, including legal team, industry reputation and insurance claim history. If the lender approves your loan but requests you to change a builder, it is probably a good thing for you.

9. <u>Sponsor or developer background:</u> Usually, lenders will prefer to deal with experienced developers, otherwise they may require the developers to hire an experienced and reputable project management firm.

10. <u>Project manager:</u> A project manager in the real estate sector is responsible for the progress and procurement of new property developments. They manage both new build and remodelling projects from conception through to completion.

In the Top 100 Rich List in Australia, and in many other developed countries, almost half are property developers. It is such an attractive business, but takes a lot of capital, skills, leadership and capability to fundraise and sell the stocks, attract tenants, obtain planning permits, etc.

There is an old saying in property development - 'If you want to go bankrupt, one of the fastest ways is to do a development project'.

Don't be too greedy. Work hard. Do your homework. Stay humble. Listen wisely. Accept uncertainty. Cope with surprise. Good luck.

CHAPTER ELEVEN

CAR LOAN TRAP!! THINK TWICE!!

This chapter aims to save you $2,000 interest or more. Car loan companies are designed to lie to consumers with complicated maths, distracting them from the real costs and side effects.

Personally, I had two car loans. I regretted this a bit because the car loan encouraged me to spend beyond my means, and yet I was still the one who needed to pay for it in the long-term.

Almost all car loan calculators online won't tell you these facts, nor will the car loan manager in the dealership, or even your banker or brokers. I was shocked that many people only found out the rates and costs are so high on the day they picked up the car.

Here are the industry secrets for car loans. Read them carefully to hopefully avoid the car loan trap.

Secret Fact No. 1: Getting a car loan first will affect your borrowing power when you are buying a property.

It is not the car loan manager's job to tell you this. They are incentivised to help the sales manager sell the car on the spot and make you feel like it is a $0 down payment deal. I've seen too many young people show up and want to get their first home loan, but the process takes at least one year because they need to pay off their car loan and save more money. Guess how much the house price goes up in a year's time? Let's say 10%. So, if a new house worth $700,000 increases 10%, you will have $70k equity, and then you can cash out up to 80% of its equity, which is $56k. The interest rate for a home loan is usually 3% lower than for a car loan. So, you are paying $1,680 less per year.

Don't teach your kids to buy a good car first. Teach them to buy a good house first. In general, house values appreciate, car values depreciate.

Secret Fact No. 2: What is my real car loan interest rate?

You may find that the car loan manager or car loan broker avoids discussing the loan interest rate. They want to emphasise the positives:

Car Loan Trap!! Think Twice!!

- Easy income verification (sometimes none)
- You can borrow up to 100%
- It is a $0 deposit deal
- We can make your monthly repayment as low as possible.

The complicated formula can make a 3% interest rate but with a high balloon more expensive than a 6% interest rate car loan with no balloon. So, what is a balloon?

Secret Fact No. 3: What is a balloon designed for?

<u>Definition:</u> A balloon payment is a lump sum owed to the lender at the end of a loan term after all regular monthly repayments have been made. This allows you to repay only part of the principal of your loan over its term, reducing your monthly repayments in exchange for owing the lender a lump sum at the end of the loan term.

So, is a balloon a good idea?

Pro: it reduces the monthly repayments and allows you to buy a better car today.

Con: You still need to pay the residual value at the end of the loan term. And the higher the balloon, the more interest you will be paying during the entire loan term.

So next time you get a car loan, don't just try to minimise your repayment; ask and compare. Get the facts on what the total interest is (not just the rate, not just the rate, not just the rate) between different options.

Secret Fact No. 4: What's the exit fee?

No one will emphasise this to you during your car loan application because they are afraid to lose your business.

If you don't ask, they won't tell you. It will be hidden somewhere in the small print in the loan contract that you will probably never read.

This can be a scary fact because:

- The exit fee is 30% of the remaining total interest
- The exit fee cannot be calculated - you will find it out later
- There is no fixed exit fee.

Which one do you prefer? I believe you prefer none of them.

Secret Fact No. 5: Term: Should I choose three years or five years?

The longer the term, the more total interest you will be paying, even if a longer one may provide you with a lower interest rate and lower repayments.

Again, don't just try to minimise your repayment; ask and compare. What's the total interest (not just the rate, not just the rate, not just the rate) between different options?

Secret Fact No. 6: Don't compare the rate!! Compare total costs over the car loan term!!

By now, you've probably realised that the car loan calculator is designed to hide things from the consumers, so remember - total costs of the car loan is the ultimate answer, no matter what tricks they play to direct your attention elsewhere.

Don't sign up for anything you cannot afford later on. Don't sign up for anything if you are not aware of the full costs.

Secret Fact No. 7: What tax benefits do I get?

For most self-employed people, if they are getting a car loan for business use, they can claim a certain portion, such as costs to offset against your revenue, depreciation, etc. For certain professions and job positions for salary earners, they can get a certain portion of tax benefits too.

It is wise to speak to your accountant before getting the car loan. It will certainly reduce your after-tax costs.

Secret Fact No. 8: Fast means expense in the car loan industry.

Many car dealers and car loan managers are trying their best to stop their clients from walking away to compare the deals from other car dealers, or banks' offers.

Their system is also trying to make it fast and easy, and some ways they do this are:

- Approve on the spot
- No need for bank statements
- It is approved too quickly for you to have the time to ask your bankers or brokers, or your accountant's opinion.

They'll give you the key, and you can drive it away now. Most will come to regret it later, like me.

Secret Fact No. 9: If you save on car price, you will pay it back on the car loan cost. Combine deals, and you get no discount in the end.

The car sales manager makes the consumers feel good about having found a bargain. But are you really getting a discount overall? You may get a discount on the car price, but then the dealer can easily earn the difference back from the car loan if you don't know all the terms and secret facts above.

I hope this small chapter has helped to equip you with some knowledge to achieve your personal financial goals.

CHAPTER TWELVE

ESTATE PLANNING WITH PETER LUMB AND STEPH CHAFER

After a ten-year career in mortgage broking, mostly acquisition of new assets, I have also encountered many divorce and estate planning cases that have not gone so smoothly. Prevention is the key for all asset protection. Firstly, many cases did not have proper or updated estate planning in place, which left the family and loved ones in chaos and dealing with an inconvenient set of circumstances. It is a pity to see that many cases conclude in the selling of all the assets and sharing the cash, missing the chance to collect future rent or capital upside. Those great quality assets were hard-earned and held for so long by the previous generation. If the parents or grandparents of those involved saw this from heaven, it wouldn't surprise me if they were so angry.

That's why I have included this chapter in my book. Please do not disregard it as irrelevant, especially when you have more and more assets and family members. Never neglect the importance of this side of asset protection. There are some wealthy families that put into place conditions that say the beneficiaries do not become entitled to all or part of their inheritance until, for example, the age of 40, when they have the maturity to deal with a large inheritance. There are other smart conditions that are often included, such as including the grandchildren as beneficiaries rather than leaving everything to the immediate family, which may offset any issues when it comes to divorce and the dividing of assets that can affect future generations. With all of the planning that you have done throughout your life, it is important to remember to plan ahead when it comes to passing on your will to future generations.

I have interviewed one of the top lawyers in town and one of his colleagues, both of whom are experienced in this area, to save you a few hundred-dollar consultation fee. Hopefully, this will plant some seeds in your future asset planning.

Peter Lumb, Associate Director at Nevett Ford Lawyers, leads their Commercial and Property Law Practice Group and provides experienced commercial legal advice to property developers, joint venture partners and investors with a focus on creating the most appropriate documentation to give effect to agreed arrangements between the relevant parties. Additionally, Peter has for many years provided estate and succession planning advice, assisting clients with appropriate wills and associated estate planning documentation tailored to their circumstances.

Estate Planning With Peter Lumb and Steph Chafer

Peter Lumb

Position: Associate Director

Practice Area: Commercial Law, Wills and Estate Planning and Probate Law

Education and Qualifications: LLB University of Melbourne

Area of Expertise: Commercial and Corporate Law, Property Law, Wills and estate planning

Professional Memberships: Law Institute of Victoria, Law Australasia

Peter is in the Commercial and Property Law Team, where he provides experience and commercial insights to the property, development, joint venture, commercial, investors with a focus on preparing the most appropriate documentation to give effect to agreed arrangements between the relevant parties.

He uses his experience to negotiate and provide and prepare transactions for both complex commercial undertakings and business and for clients for business clients, ranging from small businesses to substantial unlisted and listed offerings.

Additionally, Peter provides specialist estate planning, succession planning advice, advising clients with appropriate estate plans and interstate planning and preparation relevant to them and their estates.

Stephanie Chafer, Wills & Estates Clerk / Office Supervisor at Nevett Ford, has been a part of the Wills and Estates team for many years and it is with compassion and empathy that she is able to guide clients through the difficult and overwhelming process of estate administration. Steph provides assistance to our clients in the preparation of Wills, Powers of Attorney and other estate planning documentation.

Stephanie Chafer

Position: Wills & Estates Clerk / Office Supervisor

Practice Area: Wills & Estates / Business Services

Education & Qualifications: Advanced Diploma of Legal Practice, Bachelor of Law -Final Year-

Steph has been a part of our Wills and Estates team for many years and it is with compassion and empathy that she is able to guide clients through the difficult and overwhelming process of estate administration. Steph provides assistance to our clients in the preparation of Wills, Powers of Attorney and other estate planning documentation.

Steph is also a part of our Business Services Team and after being a part of the Nevett Ford team for over 16 years, she has obtained an in depth knowledge of the firm which allows her to implement new processes with the aim to improve the service provided to our clients.

WHAT'S THE DIFFERENCE BETWEEN MAKING A WILL AND AN ESTATE PLAN?

Peter – A will is a legal document where you appoint executors to look after your estate and you set out how what you own is to be passed down to the beneficiaries. It can be straightforward or complex. An estate plan is a process where people like us look at your family situation, overview your financial situation and suggest to you the simplest and most tax effective way to pass on assets to your family or whoever you want to benefit. The first is a purely legal document that states your wishes as to how your estate is to be distributed and the other is a process to assist will makers to comprehensively deal with all aspects of their legal and financial affairs.

WHY DO WE NEED AN ESTATE PLANNER?

Peter – An estate plan helps you make sure you don't forget things which you might do if you just do a simple will. The estate plan goes beyond it. It is a process where your situation is looked at. It is essential that you look at all the additional matters and put them into a plan where it is not just a will, but rather you look at what you own or control and make sure it ends up where you want it to end up. It is passing on control and that is often overlooked in just doing a straightforward or simple will.

WHAT HAPPENS IF YOU DON'T HAVE AN ESTATE PLAN?

Steph – If you don't have an estate plan or a will, essentially all those decisions are outside of your control. The Probate and Administration Act in Victoria decides who has the right to deal with your assets. The Act sets out how your estate is to be distributed so essentially you lose control of the decision-making.

Estate Planning With Peter Lumb and Steph Chafer

WHAT IS INVOLVED IN MAKING AN ESTATE PLAN?

Peter – The reason you need to think more carefully about what you need to deal with is there may be a whole range of different circumstances that affect people, e.g. marriages, separations, blended families, family business or assets which you want to protect. You might have children who are potentially vulnerable to claims that could result in their inheritance potentially ending up with creditors. There could also be a certain amount of tax planning that can be built into an estate plan that is more effective as to how assets are moved onto the next generation.

In terms of how we do it, we try to get some understanding of the overall situation – children, marriages, businesses, overview of the financial situation, assets and more importantly who owns or controls them. Often people think they own assets, but they are actually tied up in a company or perhaps a trust fund that may be controlled by others. Or they might have property which they treat as their own, but it could be owned jointly. So, we tease out that information to get an idea of what is needed by the will maker and the will maker's family. Once we have that, we suggest things they might need to think about in forming their estate plan and what needs to go into the will to fit in with that estate plan. One of the things people tend to forget about is superannuation and insurance which is linked to their superannuation. They might think, 'I am not worth a great deal of money,' but then when they pass on, the superannuation death benefits or insurance proceeds may not go to the intended beneficiaries if they're not nominated or appropriate provisions made in their will.

DO YOU HAVE TO HAVE A LOT OF ASSETS AND WEALTH TO MAKE AN ESTATE PLAN?

Steph – An estate plan should be considered by someone who has complex assets or is of a high net worth because it is going to reduce the risk of not being able to control where your assets are going. However, it is not just the wealthy who should consider some degree of planning; we all have assets, superannuation, bank accounts and those things need to be taken into account, so some degree of planning is needed. It is not always just talking about the assets you have now. You need to consider future assets such as a potential inheritance as well.

WHY SHOULD PEOPLE NOT DO IT THEMSELVES? FOR EXAMPLE, A POST OFFICE KIT?

Steph – Post Office kits are a set of preset questions and there is no consideration about your family situation, your assets, your debts. The premade plans do not do that or cannot do it comprehensively. If you want your wishes fully considered having regard to your circumstances, a will kit is not sufficient. Apart from not dealing with all aspects of your potential estate there is a risk that the will kit is used in such a way that there is uncertainty as to what is intended, causing problems or disputes in dealing with your estate.

Estate Planning With Peter Lumb and Steph Chafer

DO PEOPLE COME TO YOU TOO LATE TO MAKE AN ESTATE PLAN?

Peter – If you are still alive and have legal capacity it is never too late. People do put off making wills as they fear it may put some blight on their lifespan. I would say do not wait until you are incapacitated or incapable of properly making decisions to make a will; then you are in a situation where you might die without a will and have what is called an intestate estate. None of us knows what lies ahead and it is just as important for younger people, particularly with young children to provide for, to plan as it is for the older generation.

WHERE DO YOU START WHEN MAKING AN ESTATE PLAN?

Peter – It is a process of going through the family situation and financial situation. If they come to us they will get a checklist with initial information which we need to start making an estate plan for them. We then have an initial interview to understand exactly what their wishes are. To provide that information whoever is making a will needs to know and advise what they own, details about superannuation, insurance, shares, investment, details of any business they are involved in.

WHAT ARE THE MOST COMMON MISTAKES WHEN IT COMES TO WILL MAKING?

Peter – Wills using will kits can be very unclear and that puts an unfair burden on the executor which can also cause dreadful disputes within the family. It is a bit of a false economy to do that.

Another mistake is to not really understand how assets are owned. There may be things you control but they are not in your name and so they won't be included in your estate to be dealt with in accordance with your will. You need to ensure those assets that are not in your name will end up where you would like them to.

People sometimes want to exclude certain beneficiaries and there may be some difficulties about that if the estate is not planned with this consideration and explanation. A will maker might have good reason for excluding someone but that doesn't prevent that person who is an eligible beneficiary from making a claim against the estate at some later time. There are some things you can do to mitigate against claims. An explanation as to why you are excluding that beneficiary may be highly persuasive if there is a dispute down the line but people often just leave people out with no explanation which can be challenged more easily.

Another issue is that people forget about their liabilities sometimes; they might have a lot of trusts with interlocking loans. That may mean that something they leave to one beneficiary is going to be diminished because of a liability that they have not thought about.

Another common mistake is that sometimes we assume certain people are still going to be living and others may not be in terms of who we appoint as trustees or executors as none of us have any assurances of how long we are going to live. For example, if you are appointing executors it is usually not a good idea to appoint someone older, but if you do, it is also a good idea to have alternates.

People worry about the costs of getting an estate plan prepared but when you look at total assets and net worth, the cost is minimal so it shouldn't deter people from doing it if they potentially have these and other kinds of issues that requires some planning.

WHAT MAKES YOU WANT TO BE AN ESTATE PLANNER?

Steph – For me personally I have seen my own family go through disputes when it comes to deceased estates when there is actually a will in place, arguments between family members about things they are not happy with, so it breaks the family apart. Also, where there hasn't been a will and people who thought they should get something didn't because the distribution was governed by the Administration and Probate Act in Victoria. So, I can see how it can fracture a family. I am interested in this area as we assist the clients to make sure their wishes are met in accordance with what they want to the best of our ability.

WHAT IS A TESTAMENTARY TRUST AND HOW DO THESE WORK?

Peter – These are a lot more common and are frequently used in wills. It is a fact that we have recent generations in

Australia during the post-war years that have become affluent and accumulated significant assets. A testamentary trust is like putting a discretionary trust into your will but unlike the discretionary trust, which works while you are alive, the testamentary trust comes into effect when you die. People use them as an opportunity to direct assets they might have to trust funds set up under their will for each child and their children, for example. It creates flexibility for those children as to how they receive their inheritance and how they distribute to their own family. Under current tax law there is a concession for dependent children of a testamentary trust created under a will in a deceased estate where they can receive the same tax threshold as an adult. Under current tax law you can distribute income at the moment about $18,000 a year tax free for each of those children and if you are paying school fees for example, it can be applied in that way.

There are other reasons why people use these trusts. Sometimes they might have a vulnerable child who might have a drug habit, or some other reason where they can't make sensible decisions about what they might receive from you in terms of inheritance, and you can appoint trustees to manage the fund for that child.

If you have a child who might be in any profession or job where they might get sued by someone in the course of what they do, then it is not a great idea for them to receive the inheritance in their own name. If it is received in the trust via the will there is a level of protection from their creditors because it is in the trust and not personally owned by them.

This in very simple terms is how testamentary trusts work. Technically they are called discretionary will trusts and they have become a very useful tool in estate planning.

HOW WILL MARRIAGE AFFECT ESTATE PLANNING?

Steph – Under the Wills Act, essentially when you get married your will is automatically revoked. There is an exception to that if you have made your will and expressed in a clause that you have made your will in contemplation of marriage. When you flip that, and it comes to divorce or separation your will isn't automatically revoked. It is not until you are divorced that sections of the will are automatically revoked and that is when it comes to gifts to your ex-spouse or where they are appointed an executor. The lesson is that when you are getting married or divorced you need to consider looking at your will and amending it

SOME PEOPLE THINK IT IS A PITY THAT PEOPLE SELL THEIR PARENTS OR GRANDPARENTS' PROPERTY PORTFOLIO AFTER THEIR DEATH, RATHER THAN RETAINING THE FAMILY WEALTH IN A TRUST OR EXISTING STRUCTURES AND SETTING UP A FAMILY OFFICE TO KEEP GROWING THOSE ASSETS UNDER THE TRUST FOR PRESENT AND FUTURE GENERATIONS. IN YOUR EXPERIENCE, ARE SUCH ARRANGEMENTS BECOMING MORE COMMON?

PETER – I think they are, and it is a result of the fact that some families have accumulated significant wealth either through a family business, a property portfolio or by other means. There is sometimes a desire to preserve those wealth assets for future family members rather than have them just going out the door when you die to the immediate beneficiaries. In those situations, it can be quite complex to achieve that result and it's a matter for the family to balance the pros and cons of doing it. There is a tendency occasionally for some people to want to "legislate from the grave" and be too prescriptive as to what's to happen when they are not around. Invariably that doesn't work very well as there can be disputes.

On the other hand, it can be advantageous to a family group if they can come to an agreement, to preserve family assets or certain family assets for the benefit of future generations. To put that in place requires a lot of thought and the family need to all be on board (or there needs to be some level of consensus) as to how that's going to work. For instance, if you are talking about a family business, who is going to run that business. Not all family members may be appropriate to do that and sometimes that is not going to work because the synergy between family members is not always right. So, you have to try and balance that and that is a discussion that can be assisted with families and that those families need to have. They might reach a point and it is becoming more common where significant wealth can be preserved which has a lot of advantages and tax reasons as well. There may be a family agreement between family members as to how family assets are to be managed in the future. They may have a family constitution to set out certain guidelines. If the family assets are significant enough, there may even be a family office to manage those assets.

Then there is a matter of having an agreement, who runs the office, what are the rights of the other family members. This is becoming more common. You don't hear about it a great deal, but you do hear of well-known families such as the Myer family who run a family office. On a smaller scale, there are other families who are running family offices if the situation requires it.

HOW DO YOU TAKE ADVANTAGE OF EDUCATION FUNDS IN ESTATE PLANNING?

Peter – The two obvious ways are you can buy an insurance product on the market. Education bonds have been around for some time and essentially what happens is, for example, grandparents decide to put money aside for the grandchildren's education and buy education bonds where the money comes out to pay the school fees. Or alternatively, they might set up a fund in their will to be used for education purposes for the grandchildren. There could be some tax savings there. There are other tax advantages or considerations which relate to the use of testamentary trusts to hold or transfer assets. Currently if you own real estate and transfer it, duty may apply on the value of the real estate. There are certain exemptions under the Duties Act in Victoria, and one is an exemption if property is transferred out of a deceased estate to a beneficiary in accordance with a will.

Other exemptions may apply where property goes from a deceased person to a testamentary trust they have set up under their will. Exemptions are available under the Duties

Act which may permit a transfer of property to a trust or from a testamentary trust to a beneficiary without incurring duty. There may be savings there or at least existing exemptions you can take advantage of that enables a more flexible distribution of assets.

Capital gains tax always rears its head in these situations. When we do these estate plans and if the assets are a bit complicated, we like to do it in conjunction with the accountants and financial advisors that act for the client, so we get input from different sources. In relation to the capital gains tax, there may for example be considerations about preserving an exemption from the principal residence the deceased lived in if a beneficiary is considering using it as their main residence.

CAN I APPOINT A GUARDIAN FOR INFANT CHILDREN IN MY WILL?

Steph – If you have children under 18 it is important to have a clause in your will expressing who you would want as a guardian. It is not legally binding, but the court will consider it seriously as that is your express wish. The court will look at who you have appointed. E.g., grandparents, they are going to be slowing down. Do they have the capacity to look after the children? Do they have the financial means to look after your children etc? It is very important to have that conversation with the person you want to appoint as it is a big responsibility. It is important to think about, put it in your will, but not legally binding.

CAN POTENTIAL BENEFICIARIES MISS OUT ON MONEY IF THERE IS NO WILL OR IF IT HASN'T BEEN UPDATED?

Peter – The courts are littered with claims by beneficiaries who felt they have missed out. It can happen if there hasn't been some sort of planning by the person making the will or some thought given to how it's all meant to work. If there is no will, whatever you have will be distributed in accordance with the Administration and Probate Act in Victoria, which essentially is to partners, children and close relatives but it may not be the way you want it to go. A danger is in relation to superannuation benefits. When you die, if you have superannuation, there is a death benefit which will be paid to the person you have nominated it is to go to if there is a binding nomination in place. If there are no dependants or no one nominated it will normally go to your legal personal representative who if you have a will is your executor. You need to get advice from people like us if you should nominate or not nominate. Sometimes the control of superannuation benefits might fall to someone who directs those benefits in a way you don't want.

The whole point of estate planning is to minimise the risk of disputes and disagreements and maximise the wishes of the willmaker.

DO PEOPLE NEED TO DO POWERS OF ATTORNEY AND APPOINTMENT OF MEDICAL TREATMENT DECISION MAKERS?

Steph - This is something we always ask when it comes to estate planning or making a will. The importance of having a power of attorney and medical treatment decision-makers is if you don't have an enduring power of attorney there is going to be someone appointed to make those decisions for you. The same if you don't have a medical treatment decision maker appointed there is no control over who makes those decisions. Control of what you want is important and that's what those documents do. People will look after you and do what you want them to do.

CONCLUSION CHAPTER

FOR A NEW BEGINNING

It is such a relief that I have finally completed the book that I started to write five years ago. I had sold 100 copies before I even started it, which became a debt that I owe to my friends and colleagues. Every now and then they run into me and ask, 'Where is your book?' I felt ashamed the longer I dragged it out. I tried so many ways to start it, stopped for many reasons, and started again. Writing a book is certainly not easy. Work and life become busier and busier. I was not confident enough at one point as well, thinking that given I did not have a sizable property portfolio yet, should I publish a book like this to teach people how? Now I have more confidence than five years ago, but it is not just because I have more investment properties, nor because I accumulated more experience or gained more industry awards. Rather, it is due to my willingness to share and influence the industry, and I felt like 'If I cannot get this done in the next six months, I will never try to write this book anymore'.

The idea of writing a book is 'do or die'.

Many awards in the industry were given by the banks and lenders, or private institutions, to whoever was good at selling, gave them the most business – they would get the awards. The awards were judged on the number or volume of loan transactions. Yet there are no measurements of how the loan and property settlement impact the clients positively post-settlement.

For example, the number one broker in the country, ranked by MPA Broker Magazine, usually wrote more than 500 to 600 applications per year. How is that possible? It is simply a volume game – hire many administrations, like a factory, and you don't necessarily see all the clients, or maybe have just one handshake. The marketing team will pick the typical mum and dad PAYG simple deal. There are only rates comparisons, calculator comparisons, there is no financial literacy or investment education, simply because there is not enough time.

On the other hand, there are many lending managers in the banks who chose to quit their jobs because the lifestyle was not sustainable. The KPI pressure was too high. And many brokers cannot survive in the industry for different reasons.

If you look up ProductReview.com.au, you will find that most big banks get less than a two-star review. Banks' executives

For A New Beginning

still get paid millions of bonuses despite their customers and staff being unsatisfied, so long as their shareholder is satisfied. The banks are getting richer and richer; however, the affordable housing is still a social issue and becoming more severe. The numerical literacy in Australia still ranks at the bottom around the globe. Australia as a developed country still has three million living in poverty in 2020 according to Australian Council of Social Services (ACOSS).

Still, there are more marketing gurus than real financial literacy educators.

I stepped into the industry in December 2012, and now it is May 2022. Almost a decade later, I feel frustrated that almost nothing changed except I was growing older. I am too small to make a big change yet, however I am lucky that I earn enough money from the broker business, which ensures that my family, my wife, my children, my parents are financially sound.

But getting richer is less of a motivation for me now. 'How can I make a positive impact to our industry and the society?' I always wondered. I do not want to die with an epitaph that reads 'Thomas was one of the top mortgage brokers and won many awards'. That sounds like a hardworking sales guy and not someone who made much progress for our history. I would prefer the epitaph to say, 'On top of being a good father, a good husband, and a good son, Thomas was a good teacher for many, and a good industry leader. He and his team has made a significant contribution to end the poverty in Australia and surrounding countries. He created the legitimation of clause xxx, which made a positive impact on us.'

Retire On Rent

What motivates me to wake up early and go to work now, is to coach the new brokers in my company, and provide consultant services to many other brokers' firms as well. I enjoy spending a lot of time with my clients to discuss how to invest in the property market and how to retire with rent. To discuss what works and what doesn't. However, I can only service less than 100 clients if I want to service them well. So I built a team of knowledgeable and diligent brokers, who are also passionate about this industry. I created tools and a system as well, to provide great financial services to more clients through a team. If I have 20 consultants, then it is 100 happy clients per consultant x 20 great consultants = 2,000 happy clients a year. If I can create a knowledge system, a tools pack, to benefit the people that cannot come to our consultancy practice, such as other brokers firms (I do not see them as my competitors) and more importantly, a membership to professional property investors, then the knowledge system can impact over thousands and thousands of people every year.

And if I can outline all these basic principles and strategies of property investment, especially from a financial perspective, in a book, and share it with as many people as possible at an affordable price - just as expensive as buying me a simple lunch meal - hopefully it will have a prolonged impact on their life-long property investment journey. And this is exactly what this book aims to achieve - to enable you to create wealth through property.

This book is not the end, it is a connector between the readers and my team. We are working hard to create more updated industry news and tools for you for our upcoming website.

For A New Beginning

I hope to see you guys on my website too. Keep in touch and I do appreciate your constructive feedback and comments about this book.

www.retireonrent.au

(Reference: 'The Heist' by Simon Letch, Fairfax Syndicated, 10 August 2018)

Retire On Rent

(Reference: 'Banks' by Judy Horacek, Fairfax Syndicated, 2nd May 2018)

BONUS CHAPTER

HOW TO GET THE MOST OUT OF YOUR RENTAL PORTFOLIO

Never underestimate the relationship with a great rental agent team, who is professional and diligent. Here is a bonus chapter contributed by one of my property mentors, Lei Feng, of Preer Asset Management. In this chapter you will learn how to actively manage your rental cash cow.

Learn: * The secret formula making people line up and beg to rent your property. * Top 8 Insider Tactics to Rent Out Your Properties Almost Instantly. * 8 Ways to Rent Out Your Property Before Anyone Else.

As you know, the ideal property investment is one that will achieve capital growth over time and allows you to tap into the growth to continuously grow your portfolio - turning one investment into two, and two into four... But there's a problem. Two, actually. Here they are. Firstly, no one can predict how long it takes for the property to grow and what value it will grow to... And until that time, it's the cashflow which sustains your investment property. Secondly, even if your property has capital growth, you still need to demonstrate to the banks that you have enough serviceability in order to access the additional equity in the property. Hence, for you as an investor, it's really important to sustain all-important rental income, maximising your returns while minimising the risk of extended vacancies as you'll have to fund those costs out of your own back pocket.

Sadly, over the years we have witnessed first-hand the horror stories and excessive vacancy period resulting from poor marketing practice conducted by traditional real estate agents when it comes to leasing. The net result is the negative impact of your cashflow, your serviceability and thus your return. Luckily, as a fellow investor, I've been investing in property for over 11 years now, and there are some hardcore strategies and cool tactics I've learnt which helped me outsmart my competitors and lease some of mine and my clients' properties a lot quicker than anyone else even in the extremely tough times. I decided to share those eight ways with you in the hope that you too can cure vacancy problem once and for all and really enjoy the spoils of your property investment. (Pay very close attention to methods 5-8).

1. Make it visually impressive. Wherever possible, always use professional photography to best capture the visual

components that will most appeal to your market in the listing. Rooms need to look bright, spacious, and inviting, and the experts know how to 'stage' a dwelling to bring out its best features. You might think doing a professional photo is expensive and unnecessary. But remember, first impressions are everything when it comes to generating interest for your rental property. Oh, by the way, did I tell you from our experience properties with professional photos taken resulted in three times more enquiries?

2. Reasonable rent. It might seem like common sense. Trust me, when it comes to lowering your rent, it's a tough battle within yourself. One of my senior property managers used tell me that there are two major components when leasing a property. Appearance (such as photos) and asking rent. This isn't just about pricing according to market expectation when listing your property, it's also about carefully considering any potential rent reviews. Investors have the legal right to reasonably increase the weekly rent on your asset in line with inflation and other factors, but sometimes you need to weigh up whether an extra $15 or so per week is worth possibly losing good tenants over. When it comes to rental market, what we've found is that the market is very sensitive about the price. Sometimes, by simply decreasing your asking weekly rent by $5, it can generate a ton of new leads to attend the opens. Recently, I had a personal experience where I lowered my original asking rent from $480 to $475 per week and immediately doubled the enquiries. We successfully signed up a tenant in the same week. Yes, reducing rent by $5/week did cost me $260/year less in rent. But had I not tested the market and reduced the rent to a more comfortable level,

the property could have been vacant for another two weeks which would easily cost me $930 in interest.

3. Sell the location. Over the last decade, we've learnt that the vast majority of tenants will prioritise location first and foremost when searching for rental accommodation, followed by price and property suitability. Hence, it pays to really highlight all the area has to offer, in terms of things like infrastructure and amenity. Three things that really tick the boxes are: Train station, supermarket and café. Yes I know, café is a big influencer. It's a bit weird but try it next time and promote it especially if you are in Melbourne. Talk up aspects of the lifestyle and ambience a local resident can expect to enjoy, paying close attention to features that will most appeal to the location's predominant demographic, such as a strong café culture, good public transport links or well-regarded schools for the family market.

4. Don't restrict your tenant pool. A lot of times you might think you were not alienating any group but as a matter of fact you did. We call it implicit alienation. Alienating prospective tenants with headline statements that suggest some level of exclusion, will only serve to decrease the amount of people stopping to read your rental property listing. Let me give you an example. 'The perfect family home' immediately implies this is not a place that anyone without children should bother giving much thought to, meaning you've immediately lost a large number of younger renters. Make sense? Likewise, suggesting your investment is 'Ideal for sharing', or informing your audience of a 'No pets allowed' policy, will further eliminate a large portion of potential tenants. When you consider that a recent survey found over

How To Get The Most Out Of Your Rental Portfolio

63 per cent of Australian households own at least one pet, it's apparent that this might not be a great way to increase your listing traffic. And do you know with the vast majority of rental properties prohibiting keeping a dog it's not surprising to find that many pet owners simply don't reveal their pet-owning status on their application. Australian research indicates that for 11% of pet-owning tenants (mainly cat owners) their landlords or body corporate are unaware that they actually have two pets. So why take this risk while you can potentially charge more and get tenants to pay the pet bond?

5. Creative marketing strategy. No landlord wants to see their property vacant for an extended period of time. The two critical factors that cause long-term vacancies are advertising and price. Short term market fluctuations can affect the level of enquiry and there are often features of the property (or lack of them) that impact the prospective tenant's decision to rent or not rent. However, we find offering financial incentives will always overcome these. As an investor, our primary goal is maximising our income and reducing vacancy period. Therefore, it's important to 'think outside of the box' to attract as much attention as possible. If we are experiencing a property that is difficult to rent, one strategy we would normally do is to offer one week rent free. I cannot emphasise how effective this strategy is. To illustrate the point, here's another of my personal examples; four years ago, I bought a house & land package in Berwick Vic. After the construction handover, I put an ad on realestate.com. au to start leasing. Because it was a brand-new land estate, there were a lot of similar rental properties on the market at the same time. Especially next to my lot, there was another

one for rent. So I decided to offer one week rent free period as an incentive. We updated the headline on the online listing. One week later, I received a call from my property manager and she said she was showing prospects through and found out all the appliances, tap wares and even some of the carpets had been stolen. And the property was in a total mess. You would naturally think it would take forever to rent out this property right. I mean, we got tough market competitions, oversupply of rentals and now our appliances were stolen. What could be a worse situation than that, right? Anyway, just as I was about to give up, my manager rang me in the afternoon on the same day and said the same tenants went through my property, had sent their application form in and as long as everything could be restored within next 7 days, they were ok. I couldn't believe it. I guessed the key thing to motivate them to choose my one over others in the same estate was my rent-free promotion. Another variation of rent-free strategy which is also extremely effective is to reduce the asking rent by the equivalent of one weeks rent over the first 12 weeks of the lease agreement. Rather than using the tired option of 'one weeks free rent' we reduce the asking price by the equivalent of one weeks rent over the first 12 weeks of the lease agreement. For example, if a property was advertised at $500 per week, we would reduce the rent by $40 ($40 x 12 = $480: less than one weeks rent) for the first 12 weeks. This immediately increases the level of enquiry which results in the property getting rented faster. The discount is subject to the tenants application being approved and their move in date. The lease still remains at the full rate ($500 per week) but there is a special condition regarding the reduction.

6. Grab the reader's attention Let's talk about attention grabbing - one of the classic principle in marketing. Speaking of headline, don't ever under-estimate the effectiveness of your headline. (Whisper: even though 99% of property managers out there are ignoring this). The headline you choose for your listing can either compel or alienate your market in an instant. It's like the opening line of a book - if the author makes it enticing enough, you don't want to put the book down, but if it's just 'meh', you'll likely never get beyond that first sentence. 'The most affordable 3 bed luxury townhouse for rent' reads better than 'Brand New 3 Bedroom Townhouse for rent'. Here's a few that worked extremely well with us before - 'Sleepwalk to Work' - 'Fit for a Celebrity: Your Walk-in Robe' - 'Scene Stealer: A Very Impressive Kitchen' - 'Stretch Out: With An Unusually Large Terrace' - '3 bedrooms with 2 bedroom price tag' - 'Keep Your Cool: Coffee Just Around The Corner'. Anyway, you got the idea, right? Did you see it actually makes a huge difference by entrusting your asset to a forwardthinking and investment-driven property manager who not only understands the sports of property but also has a deep sense of marketing, instead of a fresh undergraduate from a traditional franchise real estate agency? I'll talk more about that in a minute. Now let's continue.

7. Timing is everything. Let's talk about December. A curse word for property leasing. It is often the quietest time for the rental property market. In case you need to rent out properties in December, I strongly recommend you sign the tenant up to a 13-month lease, so if they vacate at the end of the lease, it's in January, which is much busier. You don't want to fall into a cycle of having to find a new tenant every December

because you run the risk of it being vacant over the very quiet weeks around Christmas. Another thing about timing is that you don't want to advertise too early. While it may be tempting and intuitive to advertise your property for lease as soon as the current tenant gives notice, it's often a mistake. Always make sure you don't start advertising the property until you can legally gain access to it, and you've organised a mutually convenient inspection time with the outgoing tenant and you know it's clean and tidy. In most cases, people want to view the property as soon as they see it advertised. And you normally get most people through to your opens in the first three weeks. Don't waste the leads. Ideally, you want to sign up a new tenant to move in the day after the previous person moves out.

8. Keep a good tenant. Last but not least, once you've successfully leased out your property and secured a good tenant, you need to keep your property leased as long as possible. A sure-fire way to avoid rental vacancy is to renew a lease with your tenant. It's worth trying to keep a good tenant, even if it means forgoing a rental increase. Before you decide to increase the rental, you need to weigh up the cost of re-letting vs increased rents in case the tenant refuses to pay the increased rent and decides to move out. The cost of re-letting a property can quickly soak up the increased income generated by a small rent rise. If you have a good tenant in place, consider keeping the rent at the same level in the hope that they will stay. (Think about marketing fee, reletting fee and your interest payment to cover the vacancy period.) However, if you insist on a rental increase, here's a little tactic we always used for our own rental properties. We normally offered some

sort of gift at the end of tenants lease (such as 2 * gold class movie tickets, 1 bottle of wine or some Coles vouchers) with a 'thank you' note for being a great tenant. At the same time, we posted a formal rent increase notice to them and explained the reason behind our decision of increasing the rent. (It can be simply showing them the evidence of current market rent.) Through the law of reciprocity and positioning ourselves as a reasonable landlord, 9 of 10 times our tenants were happy to sign the new lease with the rental increase. Here you go, this strategy alone can easily save you thousands of dollars of opportunity cost. Feel free to try it next time. It works like a charm.

Now to wrap it up. Phew... You survived. I hope you enjoyed this report as much as I enjoyed making it for you. Unlike a lot of people, instead of giving you useless general information, I really want to give you real valuable content backed up by real life experiences which are actionable and implemented immediately to get you results faster. As long as you follow the simple strategies above, you are going to have a hard time messing up. Here's the bottom line. In most cases, you will find that utilising only method 1 and 2 will deliver you a very good result. However, when things get tough, you can always stack various methods in this report to make your listing stand out of the rest. As a fellow investor, I recognise the time, patience and converted effort required to manage your investment properties. Traditional Real Estate Agents are all typical in their approach of appointing inexperienced juniors who are yet to grasp the necessity for service. A lack of attention to detail is commonplace underlining that property management is not the focus for Real Estate Agents. Over the years, I have seen horror stories relating to poor tenant choices and the lack of Agent care often resulting in costly court cases between Landlord and the big brand Agents. The net result is that all these important property assets are devaluing whilst you are actually paying for their inefficient and old school management!. But here's some great news: Now you can stop being treated like a poor relation and start benefiting from first class property management.

ABOUT THE AUTHOR

Thomas Tang is an industry-qualified mortgage broker and mentor behind many young and successful entrepreneurs in Australia. A certain number of his clients have achieved multi-million assets portfolio in the past ten years through an ongoing relationship, including a few on the Young Rich List, family offices, and property development groups.

Thomas' awards include MFAA Industry Body nominated Most Excellent Residential Brokers (Victoria) 2019; MPA Top 100 Brokers 2018, 2020, and 2022; The Advisor Magazine, Top 25 Mortgage Brokers Firm, 2018, 2019, 2020, 2021, and 2022, and Eureka Award, Bank of Melbourne, 2015 Industry-qualified Mortgage Broker Mentor and many others.

Thomas is an expert in land banking, corporate debt advisory and development funding. He and his team are also super dedicated in assisting ordinary families to achieve worry-free financial status. Thomas has developed a unique system to help clients better identify the hot deals for new purchases and negotiate the rates and costs for his clients' ongoing annual review.

A husband and new father to a baby girl, Thomas has been wanting to write a book to help people achieve financial independence for over a decade. After achieving his own multi-million-dollar property portfolio by the age of 30, Thomas had a heart to help others achieve financial independence and live a life of pride, which is why he wrote "Retire on Rent". Thomas believes that the industry needs a good shakeup and knows there are many secrets that can be revealed to help people with their money and investment management.

Thomas has always 'walked the talk' and previously gave up a lucrative career as one of Australia's top bankers because he knew he was giving biased advice without doing the tailored research for clients. Taking matters into his own hands, Thomas decided to create a role and a team who make a

About The Author

positive difference to their clients and help them achieve financial freedom through property investment.

"Retire on Rent" is another extension of Thomas's dream, revealing the secrets the banks do not want you to know as well as offering simple, and straightforward strategies to establish a financially stable property portfolio.

NOTES

Retire On Rent

Notes

www.ingramcontent.com/pod-product-compliance
Lightning Source LLC
Chambersburg PA
CBHW041304110526
44590CB00028B/4239